新时代行业英语系列教材

总主编 姜 宏
主 编 胡 霞
副主编 石 芸 蒋伟平
编 者 王 晶 林巧芝
原版作者 Ian Badger

商务会谈英语

ENGLISH for Business Conversations

清華大學出版社
北 京

北京市版权局著作权合同登记号　图字：01-2021-1548

Author: Ian Badger

图书在版编目（CIP）数据

商务会谈英语 / 姜宏总主编；胡霞主编. —北京：清华大学出版社，2021.4
新时代行业英语系列教材
ISBN 978-7-302-57790-4

Ⅰ.①商…　Ⅱ.①姜…　②胡…　Ⅲ.①商务谈判-英语-高等职业教育-教材　Ⅳ.①F715.4

中国版本图书馆 CIP 数据核字（2021）第 055445 号

策划编辑：刘细珍
责任编辑：刘　艳
封面设计：子　一
责任校对：王凤芝
责任印制：丛怀宇

出版发行：清华大学出版社
网　址：http://www.tup.com.cn，http://www.wqbook.com
地　址：北京清华大学学研大厦 A 座　　**邮　编**：100084
社 总 机：010-62770175　　**邮　购**：010-62786544
投稿与读者服务：010-62776969，c-service@tup.tsinghua.edu.cn
质 量 反 馈：010-62772015，zhiliang@tup.tsinghua.edu.cn
印 装 者：北京博海升彩色印刷有限公司
经　销：全国新华书店
开　本：210mm×285mm　　**印　张**：9.25　　**字　数**：222 千字
版　次：2021 年 4 月第 1 版　　**印　次**：2021 年 4 月第 1 次印刷
定　价：55.00 元

产品编号：091248-01

序

在经济全球化和国际交往日益频繁的今天，无论是作为个人还是组织的一员，参与国际交流与合作都需要具备良好的外语沟通能力和扎实的专业技术能力。高职院校承担着培养具有全球竞争力的高端技术技能人才的使命，需要探索如何有效地培养学生的行业外语能力。行业外语教学一直是职业院校的短板，缺少合适的教材是其中一个主要原因。目前，国内大多数高职院校在第一学年开设公共英语课程，所用教材多为通用英语教材，其主题与学生所学专业的关联度总体较低；部分院校自主开发的行业英语教材，在专业内容的系统性、语言表达的准确性等方面存在诸多不足；还有部分院校直接采用国外原版的大学本科或研究生教材，但这些教材学术性和专业性太强，对以就业为导向的高职院校学生来说，十分晦涩难懂。

清华大学出版社从欧洲引进原版素材并组织国内一线行业英语教师改编的这套“新时代行业英语系列教材”，以提升学生职业英语能力为目标，服务师生教与学。本套教材体现了如下特点：

一、编写理念突出全球化和国际化

本套教材引进欧洲原版优质资源，全球化视角选材，结合行业领域和单元主题，关注环境保护、人口老龄化、贫困等时代难题，培养学生的国际视野和世界公民素养。单元主题、板块编排和练习设计与国际接轨，体现国际规范和国际标准，且反映全球行业发展动态和前景，帮助学生全面了解全球行业现状和掌握国际操作流程，夯实行业知识体系。

二、编写目标注重培养学生使用英语完成工作任务的实际应用能力

为响应高职院校外语教学改革号召，培养具有国际竞争力的高端技术技能人才，将外语教学目标由原来的语言能力导向转变为职业能力导向，本套教材通过听、说、读、写、译等基本语言技能训练，让学生完成不同行业领域的工作任务，将英语放到职场的背景中来学，放到员工的岗位职责、工作流程中来学。

三、结构与内容紧扣行业领域的职场情境和核心业务

本套教材围绕行业核心概念和业务组织教学单元，不同单元相互关联，内容由浅入深、由易到难，循序渐进；教材各单元主题契合行业典型工作场景，内容反映职业岗位核心业务知识与流程。每本教材根据内容设置 8 至 10 个单元，用多种形式的语言训练任务提升学生对行业知识的理解与应用。

四、资源立体多样，方便师生教与学

本套教材图文并茂。通过改编，在原版教材基础上每个单元增加了学习目标，明确了学生在完成各单元学习后应该达到的知识和能力水平；增加了重点词汇中文注释和专业术语表，便于学生准确理解行业核心概念；听力练习和阅读篇章均配有音频，并借助二维码扫码听音的形式呈现，实现教材的立体化，方便学生学习；习题安排契合单元的主题内容，便于检测单元学习目标的实现程度。教材另配有电子课件和习题答案，方便教师备课与授课。教师可以征订教材后联系出版社索取。

本套教材共10本，包括《护理英语》《机电英语》《建筑工程英语》《运输与物流英语》《烹饪、餐饮与接待英语》《旅游英语》《银行与金融英语》《市场营销与广告英语》《商务英语》《商务会谈英语》，涵盖医药卫生、机电设备、土木建筑、交通运输、旅游、财经商贸等六大类专业。建议高职院校结合本校人才培养目标，开设相应课程。

本套教材适合作为高职院校学生的行业英语教材，也适合相关行业从业人员作为培训或自学教材。

姜宏

2021年3月31日

前言

随着中国改革开放的持续深入和“一带一路”倡议的稳步推进，越来越多的企业、机构急需熟练掌握商务英语沟通技能的高端技术人才。以口语及书面语形式呈现的商务沟通与交流，体现的是商务活动最基本的工作内容，也是涉外高端技术人才应掌握的基本能力之一。

作为清华大学出版社引进的“新时代行业英语系列教材”之一，《商务会谈英语》是一本体现职业教育特色的商务英语口语教材。本书旨在将英语语言能力与商务情境有机结合，以典型商务活动作为教材编写的主线，以培养学生职业英语能力为目标，基于商务活动真实情境创设口语交流及文本写作的模块，通过多种练习实现该单元的学习目标，引导学生熟悉各种真实的商务情境，培养其用英语解决商务问题的能力和严谨高效的职业素养。

全书共八个单元，前七个单元各设置三个口语模块，涵盖与单元主题相关的商务会话内容，第八单元设置三个写作模块，涉及电子邮件、留言条等形式的商务文本写作；每个单元均列出与主题相关的生词和实用语言表达、英式英语与美式英语的差异及专业术语的中英文释义，单元末尾还设置了多种形式的练习题。总体而言，本书具有以下特色：

1.职业性

本书以提高职场商务英语沟通能力为目标，选取典型商务情境和商务活动设置口语及写作模块。

2.多样性

本书以国际商务环境下的商务活动为基础，体现商务活动的多样性和复杂性。

3.便利性

所有模块均配备朗读音频，方便教师课堂播放及学生课后跟读练习。课后练习形式多样，并提供多种任务情境，帮助学生举一反三，巩固提高口语技能。

本书可作为高等职业教育领域商科类专业学生的商务英语课程教材，也可作为提高职场商务英语口语能力的培训教材，同时也适用于对涉外商务沟通感兴趣的一般读者。

本书由胡霞担任主编，石芸、蒋伟平担任副主编，王晶、林巧芝参与全书的编写工作。姜宏教授作为本系列教材的总主编对本书的编写进行了全程监督与指导。由于时间仓促，水平有限，本书错漏之处在所难免，敬请读者批评指正。

编者

2021年3月

Contents

UNIT 1 Telephoning

Learning Objectives

Upon completion of the unit, students will be able to:

- make and receive phone calls in English;
- leave and answer telephone messages;
- deal with problems that occur on the phone.

Starting Off

1 Answer the questions.

1) What are the typical business phone calls which you make in English or in your own language?
2) What difficulties do you have when making phone calls?
3) If you do not understand what someone is saying, what expressions do you usually use (to ask them to speak more slowly, to repeat, to spell a name, etc.)?

Conversations A

2 Listen and repeat.

Connecting a Call

A I'd like to speak to Max Reed, please.

B Just one moment. I'll **connect** you...You're through now.

C Max Reed speaking.

A Hi, Max. Simon here.

C Hi, Simon. How are you?

A Fine. And you?

A Can I speak to Peter Safin, please?

B Speaking.

A Are you busy?

B Can I call you back?

Checking Information

A Hello.

B Hello, John. Did you get my email?

A Yes, it's right here in front of me.

B Fine. I thought it would be quicker to phone than **send** you another message. I wanted to run through some of the **arrangements** for Tuesday...

Asking the Caller to Hold

A Sorry to keep you waiting so long. Could you hold on a little longer? The **network** is very slow today.

B How long do you think it is going to take to find the information?

A It won't be long now. Right. Here we are. The **figures** you need are…

Asking the Caller to Leave a Message

A I'm trying to get hold of someone in your sales department. Are you having problems with your phone system? I was **cut off** earlier and now there is no **reply**.

B Just a moment, please. I'll try the number for you. Yes, I'm afraid there's no reply from the department. They must be at lunch. Would you like to leave a message and I'll get someone to call you when they get back.

A Thanks. My name's Baz Mechot and the number is 453980.

Making Sure You Understand

A Can I speak to Teresa Riller? I understand that she is **looking after** Sales while Marco Stam is on parental leave.

B That's right, but I'm afraid she's not here at the moment. Can I take a message?

A Thanks. Could you say that Pieter Baumgartner called and ask her to call me back?

B Can you **spell** your name, please?

A Baumgartner is B-a-u-m-g-a-r-t-n-e-r. I'm at the Rainbow Hotel in room 13.

B Is that 13, one three, or 30, three zero?

A Thirteen, one three.

B Thanks. I'll **pass on** the message.

Ending a Call

A …OK. Have we **covered** everything?

B I think so. You just need to let me know when you can send the **report**.

A I'll send you a message when I get back to the office. Anyway, thanks for calling.

B No problem. I'll wait to **hear from** you.

MY GLOSSARY

connect	v.	为……接通（电话）	arrangement	n.	安排；筹划
check	v.	核对，核实	network	n.	网络；网状系统
send	v.	发送；寄送	figure	n.	数字；图形

leave a message		留言，留口信	pass on		传递；转达
cut off		中断，切断（电力、物资供应等）	cover	v.	涉及；包括
reply	n.	回答，回复	report	n.	报告
look after		照看，照管	hear from		收到（某人）的来信；接到（某人）的电话
spell	v.	拼写；拼读			

Useful Expressions

I'd like to speak to Max Reed, please.

– Some other expressions for checking if someone is available:

Is Max Reed there? / Can I talk to Max Reed? / Is Max Reed available?

Hi, Max. Simon here.

– This is an informal greeting. More formal greetings include:

Hello, Mr Reed. This is Simon Speedwell. / Mr Reed. Hello, it's Simon Speedwell here.

I wanted to run through...

– We introduce the topic politely by using the past tense. We can also use *I'd like to...* For example:

I wanted to run through the arrangements. / I'd like to know about your travel plans.

I wanted to ask you a question. / I'd like to ask you a question.

Sorry to keep you waiting...

– Some other expressions to use when someone is waiting on the phone:

Could you hold on? / Do you mind holding?

Would you like to leave a message?

– *Would* is used to introduce a polite offer. Note also:

Would you like me to check? / Would you like to call back later? / Would you like to hold on?

...I'll get someone to call you when they get back.

– Note the use of the simple present tense in the *if/when*... clauses:

I'll call you if I can. / I'll phone you when they arrive.

I'll let you know if I hear anything. / I'll fax you if I remember the name.

I understand that she is looking after Sales...

– Language that indicates that you already have some information:

I understand that you're coming to Warsaw next week.

I hear that Pedro is moving to Singapore.

I see (that) they're going to open a new office in Paris.

...Marco Stam is on parental leave.

– Some other reasons for absence include:

He's on paternity leave. / She's on maternity leave.

She's taking compassionate leave. / He's ill.

She's on holiday. / He's left for the day.

...I'm afraid she's not here at the moment.

– Use *I'm afraid* or *I'm sorry* when passing on unwelcome information:

I'm afraid I can't help you.

I'm sorry I'm going to be late.

I'm afraid I can't find the information you need.

Have we covered everything?

– Note how we signal that a call is coming to an end:

So is that everything? / Is that all?

Anyway, thanks for calling.

– Other ways of bringing a call to an end:

Right, I'll check the details and call you back.

I think that's everything. / Is there anything else?

British	American
parental leave	*family leave*
compassionate leave	*compassionate/bereavement leave*
holiday	*vacation*

Conversations B

3 Listen and repeat.

A Voicemail Message

"This is Ann Forsell's voicemail. I'm sorry I can't take your call at the moment, but please leave a message and I'll get back to you. **Alternatively** you can leave a message with my **assistant**. His number is 0046, (that's the country code for Sweden), 01, (that's the area code), 2132. Many thanks."

Leaving a Message

"Hi, Fiona. I've been trying to get hold of you all morning so I hope you get this. Please call Sara Remondi as soon as you can. It's about the meeting next month. **Unfortunately** I can't make it so we need to talk urgently. It's two o'clock my time by the way and I'll be going home in three hours. Bye for now."

You Can't Talk

A Hello.

B Hi, John. Can you talk?

A Not really. I'm in a meeting. Can I call you back in, say, fifteen minutes?

B Sure. Speak to you later. It isn't urgent.

The Reason for Calling

A Can you hear me now? I couldn't hear you very well earlier. The **reception** was **terrible**. Anyway, how are you?

B Fine. I was just ringing to check the time for next week's meeting. Is it still three o'clock?

You Can't Hear the Caller

A Hello.

B Hello. Sorry, I can't hear you very well. I'm in a restaurant and it's very **noisy** here. I didn't **catch** that.

B I'll just go outside. Just a moment. Can you hear me now?

A Yes, that's much better. I'm glad you're enjoying yourself.

You Have to End the Call

A John, Peter has just arrived. I'll call you when I get back to London.

B Fine. I'll be here until 5. Speak to you later. Bye.

A Bye.

An **Automated** Message

"Welcome to Haznor Business Systems. This is a toll-free number. Please choose one of the following four **options**. If you are calling about an **existing order**, please **press** 1. If you wish to place a new order, press 2..."

MY GLOSSARY

alternatively	*adv.* 要不，或者	catch	*v.* 听见，听到
assistant	*n.* 助手，助理	automated	*adj.* 自动的
unfortunately	*adv.* 不幸地	option	*n.* 选择，选项
reception	*n.* 接收效果；接待处；服务台	existing	*adj.* 现存的；存在的
terrible	*adj.* 糟糕的	order	*n.* 订单
noisy	*adj.* 喧闹的，嘈杂的	press	*v.* 按，压

Useful Expressions

This is Ann Forsell's voicemail.

– Some other formal opening expressions for voicemail are:

You're through to Ann Forsell's voicemail. / You've reached Ann's voicemail.

– An informal opening:

Hi. Ann here. Sorry I can't take your call at the moment but leave a message and I'll get back to you.

It's about the meeting next month.

– Calls often begin with:

I'm calling/ringing about (your flight).

John, about (your flight to Paris)...

...I can't make it...

– *Make* is often used instead of *attend* in informal usage:

Unfortunately, I can't make the next meeting. / I can't make Friday but Thursday would be fine. / Will you be able to make it?

Can you talk?

– Other useful expressions for checking if the person you want to talk to is free, and some replies:

Are you busy? / Are you free to talk? / Have you got two minutes?

Can I call you back? / It's difficult at the moment. / This is a good time to talk.

I'm in a meeting.

– Some other reasons why you cannot take a call:

I'm not at my desk. / I'm driving. (I'll just pull over.) / I'm just getting on a train. / I've just arrived at the airport. / I haven't got my diary with me.

I was just ringing to check the time...

– *I was just ringing/calling...* is a useful alternative way to start a call:

I was just calling about the meeting next Friday. / I was just ringing to see if everything's OK for tomorrow. / I was just calling to ask for some advice.

Sorry, I can't hear you very well.

– Some other expressions to use when reception is bad:

Sorry, could you repeat that? / Could you say that again? / I'm sorry, I didn't catch that. / I'm afraid the line's bad. Did you say fifteen? / Could you speak louder? The line's very bad.

I'll just go outside.

– Use *will* when you offer or promise to do something:

I'll call you when I get back to London. / I'll be here until 5. / I'll tell her you called. / I'll make sure she gets the message. / I'll get back to you as soon as I can.

If you are calling about an existing order, please press 1.

– Some other automated instructions:

Press the star key twice. / Press the hash key. / Press 5 to speak to the operator. / Please replace the handset.

British	American
Differences in expressing time:	
Monday to Friday	*Monday through Friday*
ten past six	*ten after six*
the ninth of December	*December ninth*
24-hour clock: 9:00, 17:00	*12-hour clock: 9 a.m., 5 p.m.*

Note: In the UK both 12-hour and 24-hour clocks are used but in the US the 24-hour clock is generally used only by the military.

British	American
Some differences in saying telephone numbers:	
360-4458 = three six oh, double-four five eight	*360-4458 = three six zero, forty-four fifty-eight*
Other differences:	
mobile phone	*cell(ular) phone*
directory enquiries	*directory assistance/information*
dialled	*dialed*

Conversations C

4 Listen and repeat.

Repairing the Equipment

A This is the Maintenance **Department** of FTB Company. Who's that speaking?

B This is Jenny from the Administration Department.

A How may I help you?

B The **printer** in Office 306 doesn't work. Could you please repair it?

A OK, I'll ask a repairman to have a look.

B Thanks.

A You're welcome.

Exchanging a New One

A Hello! Can I help you?

B Hi. The shirt I bought on your website twenty days ago was broken. Can I return it back?

A I'm sorry for that, but the return time has **expired**. Can I exchange it with a new one for you?

B OK, no problem.

A **Regarding** the exchange **procedure**, I will send you a text message.

B Thank you.

A Thanks for your calling. Goodbye.

B Bye.

Returning Goods

A This is Mary's Department Store, Jack speaking. How can I help you?

B I'd like to make a **complaint**.

A I'm sorry to hear that. May I ask what the problem is?

B The dress I received isn't the one I had ordered.

A Can I take your reference number, please?

B It's MQ 8CD6. Do I need to return it to you?

A I apologise for the **inconvenience** we have caused you. Please send it back to us, and we'll **refund** the **express fee** in full.

B OK. I'll send it as soon as possible.

A Thank you. Hope you have a nice day.

Selling on the Telephone

A Hello, is this the Purchasing Department of Sky **Construction** Company?

B Yes. What can I do for you?

A I'm a salesman for ABC Company. Our company recently **launched** a new wooden floor, with good quality and relatively cheap price.

B That sounds good. Could you please send us **samples** someday?

A No problem. May I have your name, please? Is it convenient that I **come over** next Tuesday morning?

B Yes, my name is Kate Smith and I'm waiting for you next Tuesday morning.

A Ok, see you then.

B See you.

Handling Complaints

A Hello, this is the complaint office of ACB Decoration Company. May I help you?

B Hello, your employees are decorating my house. But they changed the content of the design drawing **at random**. I hope that your company can deal with this matter as soon as possible and continue to carry out the construction according to the established drawing.

A I'm sorry to hear that. Can I get your name, please?

B David Johnson.

A OK, Mr Johnson. We will check and deal with it as soon as possible and give you **feedback** in time.

B I'll be waiting for your reply.

A OK, thank you for calling. Goodbye.

B Goodbye.

Booking Courses Online

A Hello, is this Tom English Training Company?

B Yes, it is. What can I do for you?

A I'd like to book an oral English Listening Course for two six-year-old children.

B OK. What are the requirements for the teacher?

A I am looking for a native English teacher with no less than 5 years' English teaching experience.

B OK. What time would you like to make an appointment for the class?

A At six tomorrow evening, is that OK?

B No problem. I'll make an **appointment** for you at six tomorrow evening.

A Thank you.

B You're welcome.

MY GLOSSARY

department	*n.*	部门; 系; 处; 科; 室	express fee		快递费
printer	*n.*	打印机	construction	*n.*	建造; 建筑; 建设
expire	*v.*	到期, 期满; 结束	launch	*v.*	推出; 启动; 发起
regarding	*prep.*	关于; 至于	sample	*n.*	样品
procedure	*n.*	程序; 步骤; 常规	come over		过来; 顺便来访
complaint	*n.*	抱怨, 牢骚; 投诉; 不满	at random		任意地, 随意地; 随机地
inconvenience	*n.*	不便, 麻烦	feedback	*n.*	反馈信息, 反馈意见
refund	*v.*	退还; 退款; 偿付	appointment	*n.*	预约; 约定; 约会

Useful Expressions

This is Jenny from the Administration Department.

– Other expressions for calling:

This is Mike speaking.

Could I speak to Tim?

May I speak to Bob?

Thanks for your calling.

– Some other reasons for expressing gratitude for something or for doing something:

Thanks for lending me your motor car.

Thanks for doing it for me.

Thank you for sharing your tin with me.

Thank you for helping me.

I'll send it as soon as possible.

– *As soon as possible* means to do something as quickly as somebody can. More examples:

We will get the order to you as soon as possible.

We need the repairs as soon as possible.

Please make your decision as soon as possible.

Hope you have a nice day.

– This is a greeting expression. Some similar sentences include:

Hope you have a great day.

Have a good day.

Have a nice day.

Our company recently launched a new wooden floor, with good quality and relatively cheap price.

– Note the use of the word *with* in this sentence. It indicates that something has certain characteristics. More examples:

I have a jacket with a hood.

She is a beautiful woman with dark hair.

A cup of coffee please, with sugar.

I'll be waiting for your reply.

– Some other expressions to get further information:

I'm looking forward to receiving your reply as soon as possible.

Looking forward to your reply.

I will be patient for your answer.

I'd like to book an oral English Listening Course for two six-year-old children.

– *I'd like to* means *I think* or *I want*. More examples:

I'd like to be in on the plan.

I'd like to apologise for the delay.

I'd like to think it over.

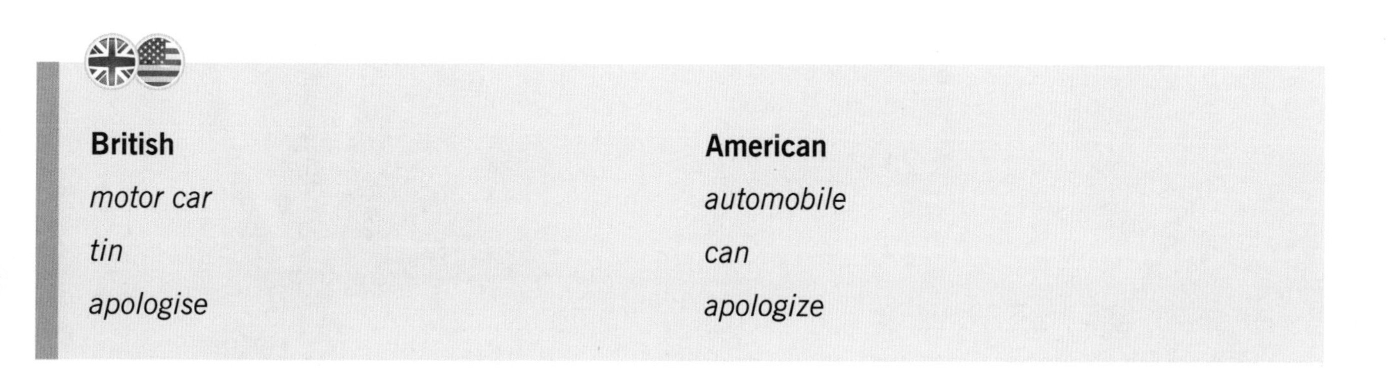

British	American
motor car	*automobile*
tin	*can*
apologise	*apologize*

Technical Terms

voicemail a system which lets people leave recorded messages for you on your telephone when you are unable to answer it 语音信箱（一种电子电话应答系统）

website a set of pages of information on the Internet about a particular subject, published by a single person or organisation 网站，网址

toll-free number / phone call a call that is free for people to make 免费电话

Practice

1 Complete the sentences using the verbs from the box below. Use each verb once only.

press	try	call	hear	leave	keep	want	say	hold	hang	get (x2)

1) I'm trying to ___*get*___ hold of Peter Ince.
2) Would you like to ________ a message?
3) I can't ________ you very well. Please speak up.
4) Could you ________ on, please? I won't be long.
5) Sorry to ________ you waiting.
6) Can I ________ you later?
7) If you ________ to place an order, ________ the star key.
8) I'll ________ someone to call you later.
9) He didn't ________ when he would be back in the office.
10) Please don't ________ up. I'll ________ the number again.

2 Write what you would say in these situations. Refer to the Conversations and Useful Expressions.

1) You are the manager. The phone rings and you pick it up. The caller asks "Is that the manager?" What do you say?

   Yes, (Tina Forget) speaking.

2) Your female colleague is off work as she has just had a baby. What do you say to the caller who wants to speak to her?

   ____

3) You are in a meeting and you receive a call on your mobile phone. You cannot speak. What do you say?

   ____

4) Leave a message on your colleague Peter's voicemail. Say that you called and ask him to call back when he gets the message.

   ____

5) You don't catch the caller's name. Ask him to spell it.

   ____

6) A colleague phones to let you know her hotel room number but you can't hear her very well. You are not sure whether it is fifteen or fifty. What do you say?

____

3 Complete each sentence with the correct preposition.

1) I'll call you ___*in*___ ten minutes.
2) I'm trying to connect you. Could you hold ________ ?
3) When are you going ________ holiday?
4) I'm calling ________ the order I placed last week.
5) Could you pass ________ a message for me?
6) I'll write to you ________ two weeks' time.
7) Tom is ________ paternity leave.
8) Please leave a message and I'll get back ________ you.

4 Choose an appropriate response.

1) What's the time in New York?
2) When will Eleanor be back?
3) Is that Tariq Meltam?
4) Is Mr Rotund there?
5) Have a good weekend.
6) Did you get my email?
7) Could you call me back?
8) Can you take a message for me?

a ☐ Sure, what's your number?
b ☐ Speaking.
c ☐ Yes, of course. Let me just find a pen.
d *1* 9 a.m.
e ☐ Yes, it's right here.
f ☐ Yes, he has just come into the office.
g ☐ In ten days' time.
h ☐ Thanks. You too.

5 Complete the sentences with *will* or the present simple tense.

1) I (give) him the message when I (see) him.

I'll give him the message when I see him.

2) I (tell) him you called.

____

3) If I (find) the information, I (let) you know immediately.

____

4) If Peter (not come back) from sick leave soon, we (need) to find a replacement.

____

5) If you (push) that button, you (disconnect) the caller.

____

6) What (do) if you (not find) Sergei's number?

____

6 Underline the correct item to complete each sentence.

1) Press the *hash* /*button*/*door* key.
2) Replace the *reception*/*handset*/*operator*.
3) Make a *toll-free*/*star*/*line* call.
4) *Here is*/*This is*/*Hello to* Anne's voice mail.
5) I couldn't *get*/*take*/*make* hold of John.
6) Please don't *hang*/*hold*/*take* up.
7) Don't forget to *turn off*/*close*/*drop* your mobile phone.
8) Did you dial the *area*/*secret*/*town* code first?

7 Match the two parts of the sentences.

1) Press the star key
2) Could you leave a message
3) I'll call you
4) Please wait. I'll just put you
5) I'm sorry, I must have dialled
6) We need to set up
7) I need to check the number
8) I'm sorry but I can't

a ☐ on hold for a minute.
b ☐ a conference call for next week.
c ☐ take the call at the moment.
d ☐ the wrong number.
e [1] to return to the main menu.
f ☐ with directory enquiries.
g ☐ for me on my voicemail?
h ☐ when I get back to my office.

8 Put the dialogue in the right order (1–13). Then listen and check.

a ☐ Speaking.
b ☐ Hi Tarmo.
c ☐ Thanks, Tarmo
d ☐ I'll do it now.
e ☐ Of course,
f ☐ Did you get my message?
g ☐ You'd like me to send directions to the office.
h ☐ Hello, can I speak to Tarmo Star, please?
i ☐ Yes that's right.
j ☐ Could you send them today?
k ☐ Yes I did.
l ☐ See you soon.
m [1] Hello.

UNIT

2 A Company Visit

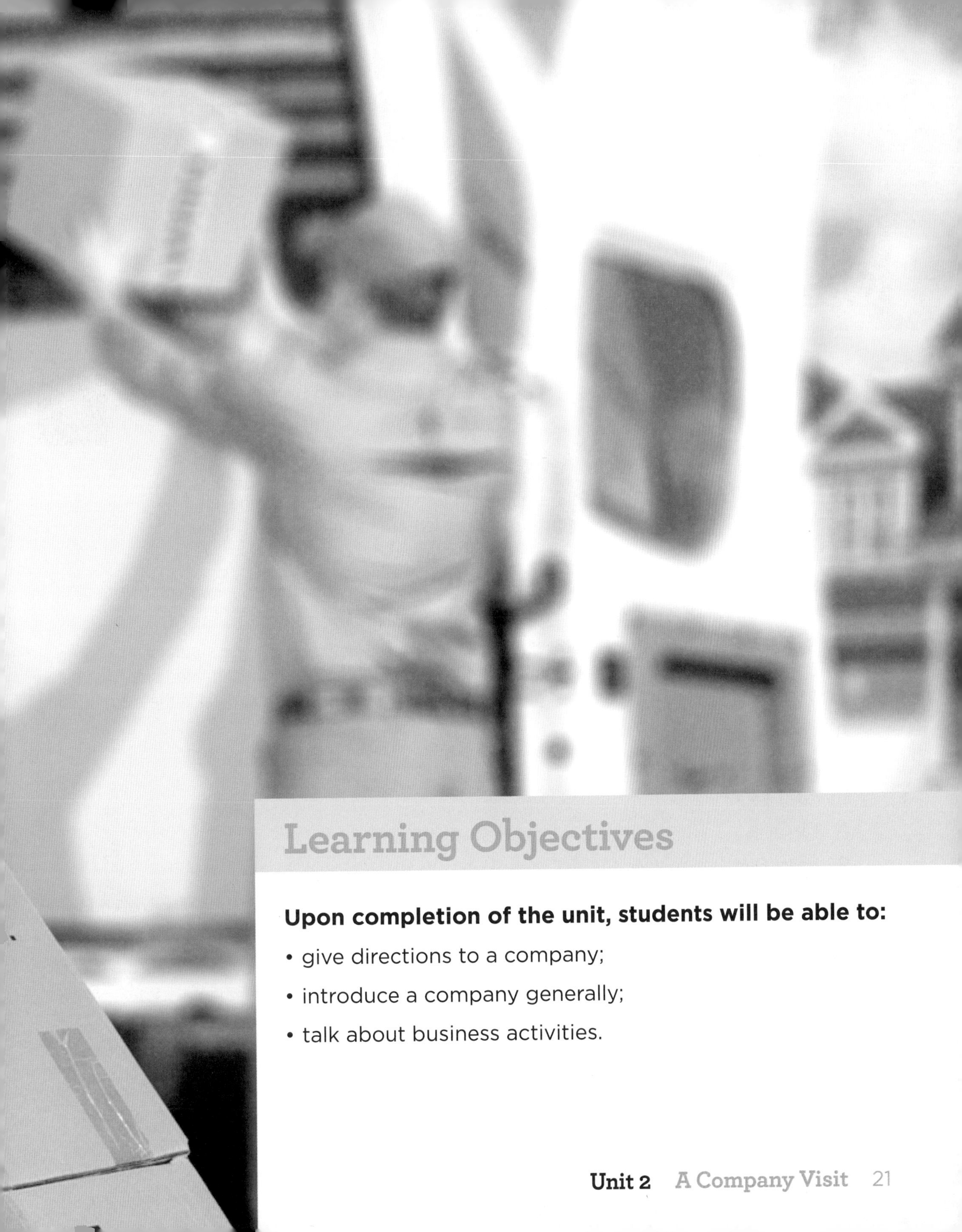

Learning Objectives

Upon completion of the unit, students will be able to:

- give directions to a company;
- introduce a company generally;
- talk about business activities.

Starting Off

1 Answer the questions.

1) Would you like to show visitors to your place of work/study?

2) What directions would you give to a visitor arriving by air, by bus, by train or on foot?

3) What is the most interesting company/school/university visit you have made?

Conversations A

2 Listen and repeat.

Directions to the Office

A Could you give me **directions** to your office?

B Just follow the **signs**. Go past the **station** and take the first turning on the left. You'll see the office on the right-hand side. I've left my car in a reserved space.

A Hi, Rosa. It's June here. I'm in the town centre outside the bus station. Could you tell me how to get to your office from here?

B Sure. Follow the signs for Frankfurt. After about two **kilometres**, you'll see a **garage** on your right. **Carry on** for another 200 metres and then turn left. Our office is on the left-hand side, just before a railway bridge. When you arrive, **park** in one of the visitors' spaces just outside the main building.

A Thanks, Rosa. See you soon.

Getting Lost

A Hi, Carla.

B Hello, Bob. Is everything all right?

A Not really. I'm lost. I'm calling from a service station on the E7 just south of a place called Melton. I don't have a map with me so could you direct me to the factory?

B Sure. Take the first left after the service station and follow the road to Porlock. Pass the shopping centre on your right and then take the first left. Carry on for three kilometres and you'll see the factory.

A Thanks.

Arrival

A Good morning, can I help you?

B Yes, I have an appointment with Hans Ekburg. Could you tell him I'm here? I've left my car in a **reserved** space.

A That's OK, I'll take the car **registration** number. Could you write your name here please and wear this? (hands over a visitor's **badge**). Do you know the building?

B I'm afraid I don't.

A OK, go up these stairs and take the lift to the third floor. Mr Ekburg's office is the fifth on the right, along the **corridor**.

B Thanks.

Meeting

A Hello, John. Good to see you again.

B And you.

A John, I'd like you to meet Lera Berman, our Marketing Manager.

C Hello, John. Pleased to meet you. Did you have a good **journey**?

B Yes, very good. The directions were very clear.

MY GLOSSARY

direction	*n.*	方向，朝向；指导，说明	park	*v.*	停放（车辆）
sign	*n.*	指示牌；标志；警告	reserved	*adj.*	保留的；预订的
station	*n.*	车站	registration	*n.*	登记；注册
kilometre	*n.*	千米，公里	badge	*n.*	徽章；像章；证章；纪念章
garage	*n.*	车库；汽车修理厂	corridor	*n.*	走廊；通道，过道
carry on		继续（前行）	journey	*n.*	旅行，行程

Useful Expressions

Could you tell me how to get to your office from here?

– We also say:

Can you tell me the way to...? / How can I get to...? / Excuse me, where is...?

After about two kilometres, you'll see a garage on your right.

– Some other landmarks:

You'll pass some shops. / Then you'll see a large red building in front of you. / Keep going and you'll come to the entrance gate.

...park in one of the visitors' spaces...

– Parking the car:

I've left my car in a reserved space. / There are some spaces reserved for visitors. / Can I park here? / Is this space reserved?

I'm calling from a service station...

– When you need to say where you are:

I'm calling from the train. / I'm on the M1 motorway. / I'm calling from a service station on the M4.

Take the first left after the service station...

– Some useful directions when you are driving:

Carry on for three kilometres. / Take the second exit at the roundabout. / Turn left at the junction. / Go straight across the crossroads. / At the traffic lights, turn right.

Carry on for three kilometres...

– Other expressions for talking about distance:

Drive on for another ten kilometres. / ...until you come to a service station. / It's 200 metres past the service station on the right-hand side.

I have an appointment with Hans Ekburg.

– Note the statements and responses:

I'm here to see Hans Ekburg. / Can I have your name, please? / Could you sign in please? / Is Hans Ekburg in? / Yes, he's expecting you.

Do you know the building?

– Checking if a visitor knows his/her way around a building:

Have you been here before? / When were you last here? / I haven't been here before.

Mr Ekburg's office is the fifth on the right, along the corridor.

– Some other office locations:

It's opposite the lift. / It's just past the coffee machine. / Go through the automatic doors.

Hello, John. Good to see you again.

– An informal greeting. Other possibilities:

Hi, John. How are you? / How's life? / How's it going?

Possible responses:

Fine thanks. / I'm very well.

I'd like you to meet Lera Berman...

– Some language of introductions:

I'd like to introduce Lera Berman. / Have you (already) met? / Yes, we met last year.

Did you have a good journey?

– We can also say:

How was the journey? / How was the traffic?

British	American
service station	*gas/filling station*
shopping centre	*(shopping) mall*
car registration number	*license plate number*
lift	*elevator*
shop	*store*
motorway	*freeway/expressway/interstate*
roundabout	*traffic circle*
crossroad	*intersection*
traffic light	*stop light*

Conversations B

3 Listen and repeat.

Introducing a Company (1)

A We're in the **label** business. We produce all kinds of labels—price labels, bottle labels, even **postage stamps**. We have factories in France, Germany, Malaysia, China and the UK.

B How many people work for the company?

A We employ just over 5,000 people **worldwide**. There are around 400 employees in this factory.

B Is business going well?

A Yes it is, and it's growing all the time.

Introducing a Company (2)

A So, tell me more about your mailing business.

B Sure. We provide a complete **packaging** and mailing service for our customers. We now have **branches** all over the south of the country and we have plans to open new branches in the north.

A What kind of company are you?

B We're a **private** limited company. We're not listed on the Stock Exchange...yet.

A What does the company do?

B We're in the **transport** business. We have an excellent **reputation** for service.

Company History

A So, how long have you been on this **site**?

B We moved here five years ago. Before that, we were in a very small office building in the centre of town.

A And when was the company **set up**?

B Ten years ago—by Simon Donna who is still the Managing Director. He started the company with just two employees.

A That's very **impressive**.

A Tour of the Office

A Let me show you round the office. Our sales **representatives** work in this open plan area. The room in the corner is Maria Krause's office. She's the **Senior** Sales Manager here. Do you know her?

B No, I don't. Has she been here long?

A No, she joined the company two months ago. Come with me, I'll introduce you to her.

A Hello, Maria. I'd like you to meet Olivier Blaireau from the Paris office.

C Pleased to meet you Olivier. How are things in Paris?

MY GLOSSARY

label	*n.*	标签，标牌
postage stamp		邮票（同 stamp）
worldwide	*adv.*	在世界各地
packaging	*n.*	包装；包装业
branch	*n.*	分支机构，分部；分店
private	*adj.*	私人的，私有的
transport	*n.*	运输；运送，输送
reputation	*n.*	名誉，声望，名望
site	*n.*	（建筑物的）地点，位置；建筑工地；（某事发生的）地点，现场
set up		建立，创立
impressive	*adj.*	给人留下深刻印象的
tour	*n.*	参观，游历，观光
representative	*n.*	代表，代理人
senior	*adj.*	级别高的

Useful Expressions

We're in the label business.

– Some other businesses:

the transport business / the paper business / the IT industry / the steel industry / the retail trade / the fashion trade

We employ just over 5,000 people worldwide.

– Other ways to talk about employee numbers:

We have just under 5,000 employees. / We have 5,000 people working for us. / 5,000 people work for us.

...it's growing all the time.

– Describing how a business is going:

The company is doing well/badly.

Things are going well/badly.

Profits are up/down.

...tell me more about your mailing business.

– Other useful opening remarks:

What does the company do? / What business are you in? / I hear you work for a mailing business.

We're a private limited company.

- A private limited company is compared with a public limited company (plc). The public can buy shares in a public limited company but not in a private limited company. Some other types of business:

  a sole trader (where one person owns the business) / *a partnership* (a business owned by two or more people) / *a family business*

...the Stock Exchange...

- It refers to the market where stocks and shares are bought and sold.

...how long have you been on this site?

- We can also talk about premises (land and buildings) and location (place):

  Our current premises are very convenient. I preferred our previous location in the centre of town.

...when was the company set up?

- Other ways to talk about the start of a company:

  When was it established? / When was it founded? / It was founded by General Kilbride in 1922.

Let me show you round the office.

- Language for guiding people round the office:

  Come with me. / Come this way. / Over there you can see the Manager's office. / This is where we handle orders.

...open plan area.

- An office area where staff members work in one large, often partitioned, space—not in separate offices. Also known as an open plan office.

...I'll introduce you to her.

- We can also say:

  I'd like to introduce you to Brit Gamlin. / You must meet Brit Gamlin. / Let me introduce you.

British	**American**
private limited company	*company/corporation*
retail trade	*retail business*
public limited company (plc)	*publicly-traded company*
a sole trader	*a sole proprietor*

Conversations C

4 Listen and repeat.

Business Activities (1)

A We're the second largest manufacturer in the country of glass for the car industry. One in three cars in this country uses our glass.

B How many plants do you have?

A We have five **domestic plants**, but we also have factories in ten other countries. As well as **supplying** the car industry, we sell glass for buses, trains, ships and aircraft.

Business Activities (2)

A Tell me more about the company.

B Basically we run a **so-called** price **comparison** website. If you visit our site, you can find links to a wide range of products and services. You can compare prices from various shops and service providers and find the best **deal**.

A That sounds very interesting, but does it really save you money?

B Yes, in my view it's much better than visiting many websites and finding the best price yourself.

Markets

A Where are your biggest markets?

B **In terms of** sales by **region**, Europe is by far the biggest market with 60 percent of our total sales. North America **accounts for** 15 percent, Asia-Pacific is 10 percent—the Chinese market is particularly strong, South America is 8 percent and the rest of the world is 7 percent.

A I think you'd better write that down for me! Why are things going so well in China?

B The Chinese **economy** is **booming** and we have a very good sales force there.

The Competition

A Who are your main **competitors**?

B It depends on the region. There are a lot of local producers in Europe and we cannot compete

with them on price. However, our reputation for service is excellent. We are well known in the market for high quality and **reliability**.

A What about the Japanese market?

B We cannot compete in Japan. High transport costs make it very **unprofitable** to do business. Maybe things will change in the future.

MY GLOSSARY

domestic	*adj.*	本国的，国内的
plant	*n.*	工厂
supply	*v.*	供应，提供，供给
so-called	*adj.*	叫作……的；所谓的
comparison	*n.*	比较，对照，对比
deal	*n.*	（尤指商业上的）协议，交易
in terms of		在……方面，从……方面来说
region	*n.*	区域，地区
account for		（在数量上）占
economy	*n.*	经济
boom	*v.*	增长；迅速发展
competition	*n.*	竞争
competitor	*n.*	竞争者
reliability	*n.*	可靠性
unprofitable	*adj.*	没有利润的，亏本的

Useful Expressions

We're the second largest manufacturer in the country...

– Talking about the size of the company:

We're by far the largest producers of... / We're the third biggest in the country. / We're among the smallest in the region.

As well as supplying the car industry, we sell...

– Use *as well as* for emphasis. We can also say:

In addition to supplying the car industry, we supply many other customers.

...we run a so-called price comparison website.

– The speaker could also say:

It's what we call a price comparison website.

These expressions show that the words *price comparison* are known to people in the business but not to others.

You can compare prices from various shops...

– We can also say:

You can make comparisons between shops. / You can compare A with B.

...in my view it's much better...

– If you are not so sure of your facts, you might say:

As far as I know, it's much better.

In terms of sales by region,...

– *In terms (of)* is a useful phrase:

What does that mean in terms of employment? / In terms of profitability, it means that... / Can you give us the figures in percentage terms?

North America accounts for 15 percent,...

– This means that sales to North America represent/are 15 percent of the whole sales.

The Chinese economy is booming...

– Some terms to describe the state of a market:

Demand is strong. / Demand is very weak. / There is a steady demand in Australia. / The market for our products is falling.

...we cannot compete with them on price.

– Ways of talking about competition:

But we can compete with them in terms of service. / Our prices are very competitive. / We've become very uncompetitive in that market.

We are well known in the market...

– Ways of describing reputation:

We have a good reputation. / We have an excellent name. / Everyone knows us. / We are well established in the market.

...transport costs make it very unprofitable...

– Talking about profit and loss:

It's a very profitable business. / We're not making much profit. / We're making a loss. / We're finally making a profit.

British	**American**
transport costs	*transportation costs*
We're making a loss.	*We're operating at a loss. / We're taking a loss.*

Technical Terms

car registration number the official set of numbers and letters shown on the front and back of a road vehicle （机动车辆的）牌照号码，登记号码

marketing the activity of deciding how to advertise a product, what price to charge for it, etc., or the type of job in which you do this 促销；推销；营销

private company a company whose shares are not traded on a stock market 私人公司，股票不公开的有限责任公司

managing director the person in charge of a company （公司的）总裁，总经理

sales representative someone who travels to different places trying to persuade people to buy his company's products or services 销售代表，推销员

manufacturer a company that produces goods in large numbers 制造商，大批量生产商品的企业

provider a company or person who provides a product or a service 供应者，供应商

producer a company, country, or person that provides goods, especially those that are produced by an industrial process or grown or obtained through farming, usually in large amounts （尤指工业品或农牧业产品的）生产者，生产公司，生产国

Practice

1 Complete each sentence with the correct preposition.

1) You need to take the lift ___*to*___ the third floor.
2) Take the third turning __________ the left.
3) Park __________ one of the visitors' spaces.
4) We are __________ far the largest manufacturer.
5) One __________ three of our plants is making a loss.
6) There is no profit __________ it.
7) Tell me about your sales __________ region.
8) We are very competitive __________ terms of price.
9) Are you listed __________ the Stock Exchange?
10) What kind of business are you __________?

2 Complete the sentences using the words in the box below. Use each word once only.

reputation	demand	profit	site	partnership	registration	~~map~~	lift

1) Could you give me directions? I don't have a ___*map*___.
2) Do you need my car __________ number?
3) How long have you had offices on this __________?
4) You can use the stairs, but it's quicker to take the __________.
5) After two years of making losses, we are now making a __________.
6) There is a growing __________ for our products in the Middle East.
7) My brother and I went into __________ three years ago.
8) We have an excellent __________ for quality.

3 Choose an appropriate response.

1) Did you have a good journey?
2) Is it a limited company?
3) When was the company set up?
4) Have you been on this site long?

a ☐ No, it's a partnership.
b ☐ Just over five years ago.
c ☐ Yes, that's right.
d ☐ Thanks, I can manage.

5) I hear you're in the transport business?
6) What kind of company is it?
7) Can I help?
8) Do you know Gunilla?

e [*1*] Yes, very good thanks.
f [ ] Yes, we met last year.
g [ ] It's a small family business.
h [ ] Yes, for twenty years.

4 Write what you would say in the following situations.

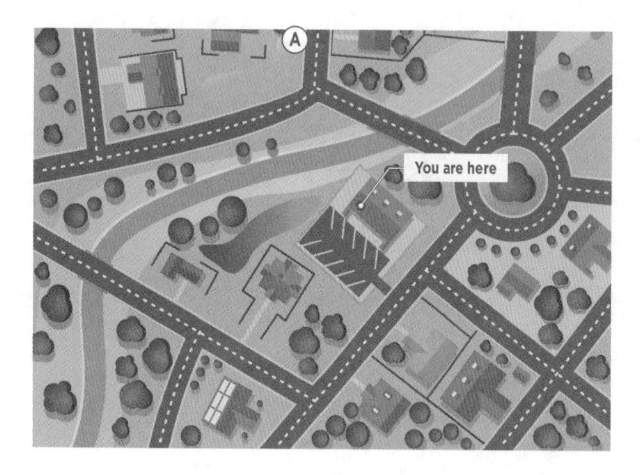

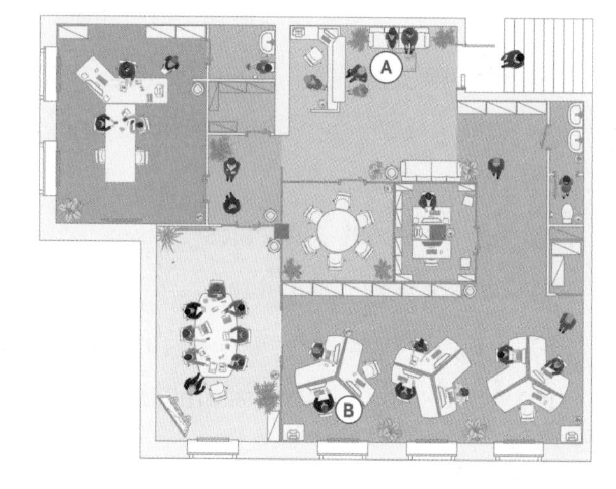

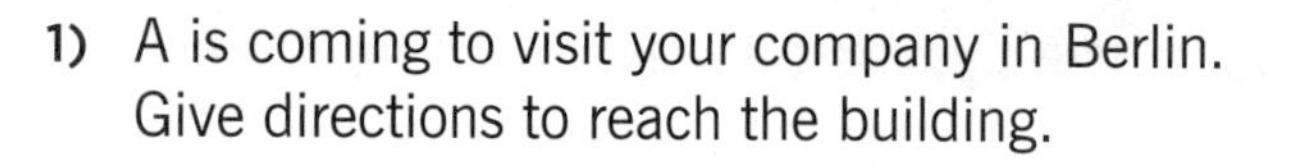
1) A is coming to visit your company in Berlin. Give directions to reach the building.

2) A is visiting B at the office. Direct A from Reception to B's desk.

5 Write down a question for each of the answers. Refer to the Conversations and Useful Expressions.

1) *What kind of business are you in?*
We're in the shipping business.

2) How many ______________________________?
We employ just over 200 people.

3) Are ______________________________?
No, we're not a partnership—we're a limited company.

4) How long ______________________________?
We have been on this site for three years.

5) Do ______________________________?
Yes, I do. The working atmosphere is very good now.

6) Where ______________________________?
In terms of region, the biggest market is North America.

7) Who ______________________________?
I suppose our biggest competitors are companies in Thailand and Indonesia.

8) Can you tell me ____?

Follow the road to Trieste and you'll see the factory on the right.

6 Rewrite the sentences in another way. Refer to the Conversations and Useful Expressions.

1) I have an appointment with Jan Pickero.

I'm here to see Jan Pickero.

2) I've parked in a reserved space.

____

3) Could you tell me the way to the main office?

____

4) I'd like you to meet our Marketing Manager.

____

5) How was the journey?

____

6) When was the company established?

____

7) We are one of the largest manufacturers in the region.

____

8) We have an excellent name in the market.

____

7 Listen to the conversation between a new employee (the visitor) and the host. Are these statements true (*T*) or false (*F*)?

	T	F
1) The host and the visitor have met before.	☐	☐
2) The visitor got lost on his way to the office.	☐	☐
3) The visitor's previous company was located in the western part of England.	☐	☐
4) The visitor wanted to change his job because he wasn't enjoying it.	☐	☐
5) The host asks the visitor to find his own way to the conference room.	☐	☐
6) The visitor speaks Russian.	☐	☐
7) The visitor previously had regular contacts with an office in Kazan.	☐	☐
8) The meeting room is on the ground floor.	☐	☐

UNIT 3

Job Information

Learning Objectives

Upon completion of the unit, students will be able to:

- talk about educational or working background;
- talk about working conditions and job benefits;
- talk about details of a job or a position.

Starting Off

1 Answer the questions.

1) What do you like/dislike most about your current job or study?

2) Can you describe your job/study history?

3) What is your ideal job? Why?

Conversations A

2 Listen and repeat.

Responsibilities

A So, what exactly do you do in the company?

B I'm responsible for new product development. I report directly to the CEO.

A What does that **involve**?

B I **supervise** a team of designers. We all have to think of new ideas, test them and develop the ones that we think will succeed.

A It sounds challenging.

B It is, but I really enjoy it.

Qualifications for the Job

A I hear you studied in Finland.

B That's right. I did a **degree** in Engineering and then I got my first job in a small **software** company in Helsinki.

A Why did you decide to stay and work in Finland?

B I was very interested in the job. The experience was really useful and certainly helped me to get the job I wanted back in Italy.

A Typical Day

A What time do you start in the mornings?

B I **aim** to get to work by 8 a.m. That means leaving home at 7:30. I usually cycle to work.

A Are the hours **flexible**?

B In theory, yes, but I normally finish at 4 p.m. I sometimes finish earlier if I take a very short lunch break.

A Do you go out for lunch?

B **Occasionally**, but I like eating in the company **canteen**.

Discussing a New Appointment

A What kind of person are we looking for?

B We want someone who is already working as a Project Manager. He or she should have at least three years' experience.

A What sorts of skills are needed?

B Excellent **communication** skills are **essential**. The person we appoint will have a lot of direct **contact** with **clients**—we need someone who can present the company clearly.

A **Absolutely**. So where can we find this person?

B I think we should **advertise** with an online **recruitment** agency, but we may have to use a firm of head-hunters.

MY GLOSSARY

responsibility	*n.*	职责；责任	supervise	*v.*	管理；监督
involve	*v.*	包含；涉及	qualification	*n.*	资格证书；合格证明

degree	*n.* 学位	essential	*adj.* 必要的，必不可少的
software	*n.* （计算机）软件	contact	*n.* 联系，联络
aim	*v.* 打算，计划	client	*n.* 客户；顾客
flexible	*adj.* 可变动的；灵活的	absolutely	*adv.* 完全地；绝对地
occasionally	*adv.* 偶尔，间或	advertise	*v.* 登广告，做广告
canteen	*n.* 食堂，餐厅	recruitment	*n.* 招聘，招收
communication	*n.* 交流，沟通		

Useful Expressions

I'm responsible for new product development.

– We can also say:

I'm in charge of new product development. / New product development is my responsibility.

I report directly to the CEO.

– This means *the CEO is my boss.*

CEO = Chief Executive Officer / CFO = Chief Financial Officer / MD = Managing Director

What does that involve?

– Notice that we use the *-ing* form of the verb after *involve*:

It involves attending a lot of meetings. / It involves working long hours.

It sounds challenging.

– *Challenging* means demanding and tough.

The job is a challenge. / I enjoy challenges.

I hear you studied in Finland.

– Note how *hear*, *understand* and *believe* are used in conversations:

I understand you spent some time in Japan. / I believe you know Don quite well.

– Possible responses:

That's right. / Not really. / Yes, I was there for two years. / Yes, we're very good friends.

I did a degree in Engineering...

– Other ways of describing studies:

I did a B.A. (Bachelor of Arts) / I studied for an MSc. (Master of Science) / I completed my studies last year. / I graduated from Oxford University in 1999.

I was very interested in the job.

– Note the prepositions:

to be interested in / keen on / fascinated by

I usually cycle to work.

– Other ways of getting to work—note the correct prepositions:

I walk / go on foot.

I drive / go by car.

I take the train / go by train.

Are the hours flexible?

– Phrases to talk about flexible working:

I work flexible hours. / We have a flexitime system.

...I like eating in the company canteen.

– Another person may prefer to have a *takeaway* or to eat:

in a local restaurant. / at his or her desk. / in a sandwich bar. / from a market stall.

Excellent communication skills are essential.

– Some key qualifications for a job:

We need someone who is very reliable. / We're looking for someone with strong leadership skills. / We want someone with a good track record.

Absolutely.

– In UK speech, *absolutely* means *I agree* or *You're right*.

British	**American**
flexitime	*flextime*
takeaway	*takeout*

Conversations B

3 Listen and repeat.

Working Conditions

A Are you pleased you moved to the Bangkok office?

B Yes, I am. The **atmosphere** is very relaxed and I have a good group of **colleagues**. There's a great mix of **nationalities** and we often go out for dinner or for a drink after work. Everyone is on first name terms.

A Don't you find it very hot there?

B Bangkok is hot, yes, but the offices are very comfortable. All the buildings and cars are air-conditioned. I have no regrets about moving.

Financial Rewards

A What kind of salary do you think we should offer for the new Sales Manager's job in Almaty?

B It's difficult to say. We would normally pay $75,000 a year plus **commission** for a job with these responsibilities, but I don't know about the cost of living in Kazakhstan and I have no idea about the level of local salaries.

A Neither have I. I'll talk to Balgira Karakas about it. She's **originally** from Almaty—I think she's working in our Dacca office at the moment.

Job Benefits

A How's the new job?

B I'm very happy with it. The salary is reasonable—not quite as good as in the last job but the company really looks after its people.

A How do you mean?

B Well, I have free use of the company gym and health club, they pay for my phone and I get excellent **medical insurance**. **Sickness pay** and holidays are very good and the **promotion prospects** are excellent.

A You're lucky.

B Yes, I am—they even give us a season ticket for the local football team!

Retirement and Redundancy

A How has the **takeover affected** the company?

B Well, the new owners are going to **close down** a plant in Manila and another in Dubai. About 300 people are going to lose their jobs.

A That's terrible.

B Actually it's not quite as bad as it seems. Most of the staff will be offered jobs in other plants and quite a few want to take early retirement.

A So there are no **compulsory** redundancies?

B Very few.

A That's good news.

MY GLOSSARY

atmosphere	*n.*	气氛，氛围；环境
colleague	*n.*	同事，同僚
nationality	*n.*	国籍
financial reward		报酬
commission	*n.*	佣金；提成
originally	*adv.*	原本，起初
medical insurance		医疗保险
sickness pay		病假津贴
promotion	*n.*	提升，晋升
prospect	*n.*	可能性；前景；预期
retirement	*n.*	退休
redundancy	*n.*	裁员，解雇；人浮于事
takeover	*n.*	接管；收购
affect	*v.*	影响；侵袭
close down		关闭；倒闭，停业
compulsory	*adj.*	必须做的；强制性的

Useful Expressions

The atmosphere is very relaxed...

– The working atmosphere can be *formal* or *informal*. It can also be *stressful* or *relaxed*.

Everyone is on first name terms.

– In an informal environment, staff are probably *on first name terms*—they use first names rather than surnames.

Don't you find it very hot there?

– Note that the use of *Don't* at the beginning of this question expects the answer *Yes*. If the answer is *No*, the speaker must emphasise the answer, for example: *Not really. / No, not at all*.

I have no regrets about moving.

– Other ways of expressing feelings:

I don't regret moving here at all. / I'm happy to be here. / I'm very pleased I moved.

...$75,000 a year plus commission...

– *Commission* is the payment made to sales people depending on how much they sell.

...the cost of living...

– The *cost of living* is the expense of living in a country. The *standard of living* is how well you can live in a country.

...the level of local salaries.

– *Salaries* are normally paid monthly. *Wages* are normally paid weekly.

Neither have I.

– Note the word order after *neither*:

I didn't go to university. Neither did I.

I'm not going to move. Neither am I.

– *So* follows the same rule:

I studied in Moscow. So did I.

I'm moving to Tashkent. So am I.

...the company really looks after its people.

– Expressions for describing your employer:

It's a great/terrible company to work for.

I have a very good / an awful boss.

...I have free use of the company gym...

– Some other benefits (if you are lucky!):

They pay for all my phone calls. / I get excellent medical insurance. / I have a good daily allowance.

...the promotion prospects are excellent.

– This means the speaker has a very good chance of getting a better paid job with more responsibility in the company.

How has the takeover affected the company?

– Note the use of the verb *affect*.

How has the takeover affected you? Compare: *What has been the effect of the takeover on the company?*

About 300 people are going to lose their jobs.

– This is more neutral than:

They are going to fire/sack fifty people.

Fifty people are going to be fired/sacked.

...quite a few want to take early retirement.

– We *take* early retirement. Other expressions:

I'd like to retire early. / I'm not looking forward to retirement.

...there are no compulsory redundancies.

– Note how we talk about redundancy:

Most of the redundancies will be voluntary.

British	American
football team	*soccer team*
compulsory	*mandatory*
redundancies	*layoffs*
to be made redundant / to be laid off	*to be laid off*
I didn't go to university	*I didn't go to college*
I have a good daily allowance	*I have a good per diem*
to sack	*to fire/dismiss (also used in British English)*

Note: *To fire* is less formal than *to dismiss* in both British and American English.

Conversations C

4 Listen and repeat.

Orientation

A Would you please make a brief introduction about the orientation for **newbies** in our company?

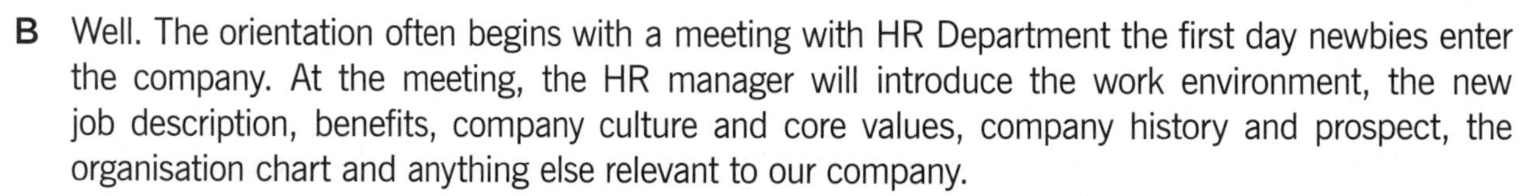

B Well. The orientation often begins with a meeting with HR Department the first day newbies enter the company. At the meeting, the HR manager will introduce the work environment, the new job description, benefits, company culture and core values, company history and prospect, the organisation chart and anything else relevant to our company.

A How is the orientation usually made?

B When the newbies enter the company, they will get the orientation **agenda** and employee handbook. HR Department will **designate** one **mentor** to help them get familiar with their work as soon as possible.

Dress Code

A Do you think the staff should always wear formal clothes in workplace?

B It depends. If you need to contact with customers or **investors** directly on some formal occasions, you'd better dress formally, because it makes you look neat and **trustworthy**. Other than that, you can wear something smart, and make yourself clean and tidy at work.

A I see. What kinds of clothes are not suitable in workplace?

B Tight or **revealing** clothes such as miniskirts don't belong in workplace. In addition, your hair and nails should be neat and clean and your shoes must be in good condition. If you look **unkempt**, your boss and coworkers may **perceive** you as someone who is careless and doesn't pay much attention to details.

Teleworking

A I have **convinced** my boss to turn my current job into a teleworking position.

B Congratulations. Working at home two or three days a week can save time and money of commuting to work.

A Certainly. It also helps to improve my **productivity** and focus on my work without **distractions** in the office.

B Furthermore, it's particularly beneficial for those who want more opportunities for **refresher** courses in future.

A You're right.

Job Sharing

A I feel tired for my work especially after I had a baby. It's difficult for me to balance my work and my family.

B Why don't you choose job sharing with a partner? Many female colleagues around me chose to share job in order to spend more time with their children.

A I'm still **hesitating**. You know, it's difficult to find a **reliable** partner.

B That's true. You must make plans together, set goals and communicate with each other effectively.

A But there are advantages of sharing job with a coworker.

B I can't agree more. Both of us can benefit from the increased **flexibility**, which gives us experience of balancing between work and life and makes us less stressed and more effective when we are working.

MY GLOSSARY

orientation	*n.*	入职培训; 情况介绍
newbie	*n.*	新手; 职场新人
agenda	*n.*	议事日程; (会议的)议程
designate	*v.*	指定, 选定; 委派
mentor	*n.*	导师; 指导者
investor	*n.*	投资者
trustworthy	*adj.*	值得信任的, 可信的, 可靠的
revealing	*adj.*	袒胸露背的; 有启迪作用的
unkempt	*adj.*	不整洁的, 凌乱的, 没有打理的
perceive	*v.*	认为, 看待, 视为
convince	*v.*	说服; 使相信, 使信服
productivity	*n.*	生产率
distraction	*n.*	分心的事; 分散注意力的东西
refresher	*n.*	进修课程; 补习课程
hesitate	*v.*	犹豫, 踌躇
reliable	*adj.*	可信赖的; 可靠的
flexibility	*n.*	灵活性; 弹性; 适应性

Useful Expressions

Would you please make a brief introduction about...?

– We can also say:

Would you like to briefly introduce...? / Could you introduce...briefly? / I wonder if you could make a brief introduction about...

It depends.

– *It depends* means it is not decided yet, for example:

Are you going to Emma's party? / I don't know, it depends. (We might be going away that weekend.) / I might not go. It depends on how tired I am. (I might not go if I feel tired.)

...you'd better dress formally,...

– *Had better do something* means it would be good to do something, for example:

I'd better leave a note so they'll know I'll be late.

You had better drive slowly and carefully.

You had better get a doctor to pull out your bad tooth.

Other than that,...

– *Other than something* means except something, for example:

The form cannot be signed by anyone other than yourself.

I don't know any French people other than you.

There's nothing on TV tonight, other than the usual rubbish.

We're going away in June but other than that I'll be here all summer.

Tight or revealing clothes such as miniskirts don't belong in workplace.

– It is not suitable to wear tight or revealing clothes such as miniskirts in workplace. *Belong* means to be in the right or suitable place, for example:

This table belongs in the sitting room.

Where do these spoons belong?

It also helps to improve my productivity...

– Other sentences with *help (sb) (to) do:*

The $10,000 loan from the bank helped her (to) start her own business.

I feel that learning English will help improve my chances of promotion at work.

Why don't you choose job sharing with a partner?

– Other expressions used to make suggestions:

Why don't you come with us? / Why don't you ask him for his advice? / Why not use my car? You'll fit more in. / If you love each other, why not get married?

I'm still hesitating.

– Expressions with similar meaning:

I'm still not sure about it. / I haven't made decision yet. / I'm still thinking about it.

I can't agree more.

– It means completely or totally agree. Similar expressions include:

I totally agree with you. / I couldn't agree more. / I fully agree with you.

British	**American**
certainly	*sure*
in future	*in the future*
smart	*well-dressed*

Technical Terms

CEO abbreviation for chief executive officer: the person with the most important position in a company 首席执行官

project manager someone whose job is to plan a piece of work or activity and organise the work of all the people involved in it 项目经理，项目管理人

head-hunter (headhunter) a person who tries to persuade someone to leave his/her job by offering that person another job with more pay and a higher position 猎头；物色人才的人

medical insurance insurance for the cost of medical treatment if you are ill or injured, often paid for by companies for their employees 医疗保险

HR abbreviation for human resources, which is the department of an organisation that deals with finding new employees, keeping records about all the organisation's employees, and helping them with any problems 人事部，人力资源部

teleworking the activity of working at home while communicating with your office by phone or email 远程办公

job sharing dividing the duties and the pay of one job between two people who work at different time during the day or week （两人）分担一份工作

Practice

1 Complete the sentences and then put them in the grid. The letters in the tinted panel will spell a key word.

1) You don't need to pay. Use of the gym is ___*free*___.
2) Is the cost of __________ high in Norway?
3) We need a person with __________ communication skills.
4) There is a good __________ of nationalities in the office.
5) Are you planning to take early __________?
6) I understand some __________ will be lost after the takeover.
7) Do you know the __________ of local salaries?
8) My employer provides free __________ insurance.

1) F R E E
2)
3)
4)
5)
6)
7)
8)

2 Complete the sentences with the correct form of the words in brackets.

1) John is now Head of *Recruitment*. (recruit)
2) Because of the factory closure, 500 people are going to be made __________. (redundancy)
3) I'm in charge of __________. (develop)
4) The company provide free motor __________. (insure)
5) I'm planning to __________ next year. (retirement)
6) It is a very __________ place to work. (stress)
7) Do you know who the new __________ of the company is? (own)
8) We need a manager with excellent __________ skills. (lead)
9) I have good __________ prospects in my new job. (promote)
10) It's a very __________ job with a wide range of __________. (challenge, responsible)

3 Choose an appropriate response.

1) I understand Frank used to work in Japan.
2) How are you?
3) I usually walk to work.
4) Did you have a good journey?
5) I don't have any regrets about moving.
6) Is it a good place to work?
7) Are you looking forward to retirement?

a ☐ Fine, thanks.
b ☐ Yes, the directions were very clear.
c ☐ At 4 p.m.
d ☐ Yes, I am.
e *1* That's right, it was five years ago.
f ☐ Neither do I.
g ☐ It can be.

8) When did you graduate?
9) What time do you leave work?
10) We need someone who is very reliable.

h ☐ Absolutely!
i ☐ So do I.
j ☐ In 2001.

4 Complete each sentence with the correct preposition.

1) I'm in charge ___*of*___ IT Services.
2) I'm responsible ________ recruitment.
3) I report ________ the Human Resources Director.
4) I take care ________ everyday office procedures.
5) I studied ________ my degree at Edinburgh University.
6) I have no regrets ________ taking my current job.
7) Isn't the cost ________ living very high?
8) I have recently moved ________ the Milan office.
9) I have been working in our Bristol office ________ December 2015.
10) I have free use ________ the company sports facilities.
11) The company pay ________ all my travel expenses.
12) How do you get to work? ________ foot or ________ bicycle?

5 Complete the crossword.

Across

1) I work for a recruitment ________.
3) I don't have time to eat in a restaurant at lunchtime. I usually have a ________.
5) The meals in the staff ________ are excellent.
7) I used to be paid ________, now I'm paid monthly.
8) I can't afford to live here. The ________ of living is too high.

Down

2) She is an Oxford University ________.
4) The company provides a very good daily ________ for living expenses.
6) The company has changed enormously since the ________.
9) "I'm moving to Istanbul next year." "Really? ________ am I!"

6 Match the two parts of the sentences.

1) I graduated
2) I report
3) I studied
4) I go to work
5) We need to advertise
6) We offered her a salary of $60,000
7) The company looks
8) I'm looking forward

a ☐ for a degree in Business Administration.
b ☐ by car.
c ☐ plus commission.
d ☐ to early retirement.
e ☐ in the local newspaper.
f ☐ to the Chief Project Manager.
g ☐ after its staff well.
h [1] from university five years ago.

7 Respond to the statements with *so* or *neither*.

1) I'm going to lose my job.
   So am I.
2) I went to University in France.
   ______
3) I'm not going out this evening.
   ______
4) I usually start at 8:00 a.m. in the morning.
   ______
5) I don't like eating in the company canteen.
   ______
6) I wasn't interested in my previous job.
   ______
7) I was very happy in Thailand.
   ______
8) I'm in the paper industry.
   ______

8 Listen to the extract from a job interview and answer the questions.

1) Which markets was the interviewee responsible for?
2) Which languages does she speak?
3) How long did she live in Brazil?
4) How often did she have contact with the Logistics department in her previous company?
5) How does the interviewer define "hauliers"?

UNIT

4 Presentations

Learning Objectives

Upon completion of the unit, students will be able to:

- start, continue or end a presentation appropriately;
- describe figures or trends in charts accurately;
- give a presentation successfully.

Starting Off

1 Answer the questions.

1) What types of presentations do you have to give? Formal presentations? Informal presentations to groups of colleagues / fellow students?

2) What do you usually need for a successful presentation? Whiteboard with a list of topics? Computer and projector? What else?

3) What are your top tips for a successful presentation?

Conversations A

2 Listen and repeat.

Getting Started

Hello everyone. It's good to see you all here so early in the morning. My name's Hiro Rosado and I'd like to talk about how we **organise** language training here. First I'll describe the **importance** of English for **internal** communications in our company, then I'll outline our study programmes for managers. Finally I'd like to say something about our plans to **outsource** this training in the future.

Moving On

...so that's all I wanted to say about the **budget** for next year. I'd now like to move on to the question Rosa raised earlier.

...That leads me to my next point. We need to look carefully at how we plan for next year...So, next year's budget. I'd now like to talk about the action we are taking to reach our **targets**.

Dealing with Questions

A How much is the project going to cost?

B I'm afraid I can't say at the moment.

C Can you tell us when the report will be ready?

B I hope to have it ready by the end of the week.

D Are you planning to **recruit** more staff?

B Sorry, I didn't catch the question. Could you repeat it, please?

D Sorry, I'd like to know if you are planning to recruit more staff.

B Did everyone hear that? The question was: "Are we planning to recruit more staff?"

Dealing with the Unexpected

A Oh, dear.

B Is it broken?

A Yes, the **bulb** is broken. I'm afraid I won't be able to use the **projector**. Could you bear with me, I have some paper copies in my **briefcase**.

B Are you OK?

A Yes, I think so. Could I have a glass of water? That's better. Sorry, where was I?

B You were just about to tell us some interesting news.

Recapping

As I **mentioned** earlier, we hope to finish the project by the end of the year. I said that we were on **schedule**. Having said that, there are a couple of **potential** problems...

Coming to an End

I'd like to finish by thanking you all for attending this **webinar** and I look forward to welcoming you to our next session in two weeks' time. If anyone has any questions, please ask. **In the meantime** you are very welcome to contact me if you have any queries.

MY GLOSSARY

organise	*v.*	安排；组织
importance	*n.*	重要性
internal	*adj.*	内部的；体内的
outsource	*v.*	外包，（将……）外包
budget	*n.*	预算
target	*n.*	目标
recruit	*v.*	招聘，招收
bulb	*n.*	电灯泡
projector	*n.*	（电影）放映机；投影仪
briefcase	*n.*	公文包
recap	*v.*	扼要重述；摘要说明；概括
mention	*v.*	提及，说到
schedule	*n.*	计划表；日程安排表
potential	*adj.*	潜在的，可能的
webinar	*n.*	网络研讨会；在线会议
in the meantime		在此期间；与此同此

Useful Expressions

It's good to see you all here...

– Speaker's opening remarks to an audience:

I'm very pleased to be here. / I'm glad you could all make it. / Thanks for inviting me. / Thank you (all) for coming. / I'm glad to see so many of you here today.

...I'd like to talk about...

– Other common expressions for starting off a presentation:

I'm planning to tell you about... / Today I'd like to introduce... / I'd like to start by saying something about...

First I'll describe...

– Expressions for describing the structure of a talk:

Then I'll discuss our study programmes. / After that I'll come to the main point. / Finally I'd like to say something about...

...that's all I wanted to say...

– Note how the speaker finishes off a section of the talk. Some other expressions:

Are there any questions so far? / Moving on to my next point... / To summarise what I have said so far...

That leads me to my next point.

– Announcing a new point in a presentation:

I'd now like to move on Rosa's question. / Moving on to Rosa's question... / Now I'd like to talk about...

So, next year's budget.

– You can sometimes simply announce a new topic or presentation slide as follows:

So, sales in Canada. These have been... / OK, development plans for next year. These are... / Study programmes. Have a look at...

I'm afraid I can't say...

– Useful expressions when you do not know the answer to a question:

I'm sorry, I don't know the answer. / I'll have to check for you. / I'm not the best person to answer that. / You need to speak to...

...I didn't catch the question.

– When you can't hear something:

Could you repeat the question? / Could you say that again? / Sorry, what did you say?

Could you bear with me...

– A very useful expression when you need time to check or find something. Alternatives:

Excuse me for a moment. / Just a moment. / Can you give me two minutes?

Sorry, where was I?

– If you are distracted or forget what you wanted to say. Other possibilities:

Can anyone help me? / Let me think.

You were just about to tell us...

– Helping the speaker to remember the point he/she wanted to make!

You were talking about the schedule.

As I mentioned earlier,...

– Useful language for recapping (summarising/reviewing) what was said earlier in the presentation:

As I pointed out / mentioned earlier...

As I said before...

I'd like to finish by thanking you all...

– Language for ending a talk:

Thank you. / Thank you for inviting me. / Are there any questions?

...you are very welcome to contact me...

– Asking the audience to contact you:

I'd be very happy to hear from you. / I'd welcome your feedback.

British	**American**
organise	*organize*
organisation	*organization*
study programmes	*study programs*
schedule /ˈʃedjuːl/, /ˈskedjuːl/	*schedule* /ˈskedʒəl/

Conversations B

3 Listen and repeat.

Some Facts and Figures

Turnover rose in the year to April by 11 percent to 4 billion dollars compared with 3.8 billion in the previous year. **Profits** jumped by 20 percent in this period. However, these results give a **misleading picture** as the company sold its French **subsidiary** during the period for a "**one-off**" profit of half a billion dollars.

Predictions

A We're currently **predicting** a **slowdown** in sales for next year. Global trading conditions are not promising. However, one area where we expect growth to continue is in Japan and Korea, where analysts are **forecasting** an upturn in the market.

B Is that for the whole of the region?

A Yes, we're looking at a growth rate of between 1 and 3 percent in these areas.

Trends: Upwards ↑

As you can see from the graph, sales have increased **considerably** this year. The beginning of the year was poor, but sales **picked up** in February and reached a **peak** in August. Since then they have fallen a little but the overall trend is upwards. The outlook is very healthy.

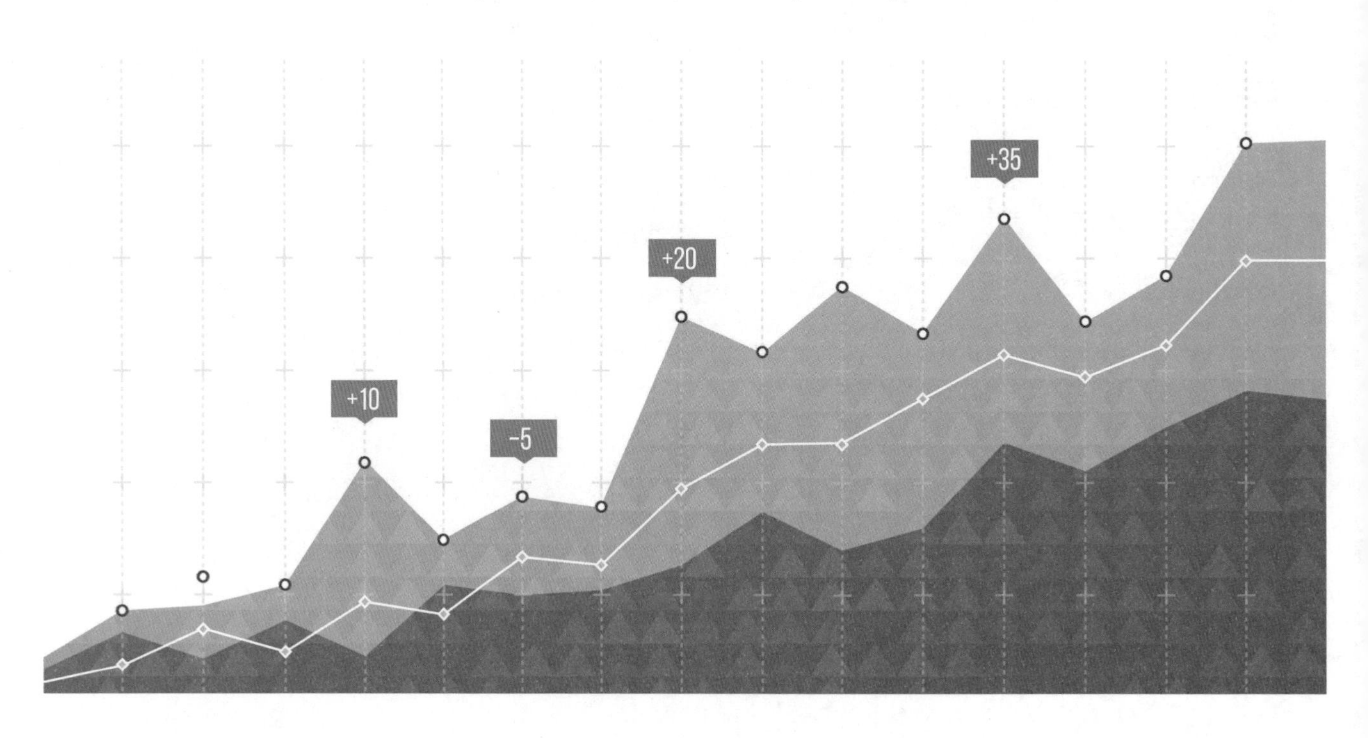

Trends: Downwards ↓

The chart clearly shows the **dramatic** fall in production since the beginning of the year, and unfortunately this is a trend which will continue. The **closure** of our Geneva plant in January accounts for the sharp fall at that time and as sales have continued to **decline**, we have had to **temporarily** shut down a number of our factories. These are difficult times for the company.

Trends: Steady -

If you compare this six-month period with the previous six months, you will notice that there has been very little change in the number of guests visiting our hotel. In fact, guest numbers have not increased for three years. We need to think about what we can do to make our hotel more popular.

MY GLOSSARY

turnover	*n.* 营业额；成交量	considerably	*adv.* 相当地，非常
profit	*n.* 利润，盈利	pick up	回升；改善
misleading	*adj.* 误导的，引入歧途的	peak	*n.* 最高点，峰值
subsidiary	*n.* 子公司，附属公司	dramatic	*adj.* 急剧的；戏剧性的
one-off	*adj.* 一次性的	closure	*n.* 停业；倒闭
predict	*v.* 预言，预料	decline	*v.* 下降；衰落
slowdown	*n.* 减速，减缓	temporarily	*adv.* 临时地
forecast	*n.* 预测，预报		

Useful Expressions

Turnover rose in the year to April...

– Other ways of describing financial periods of time:

In the first/second/final quarter...

In the year to date...

In the current year...

...by 11 percent...

– Note the use of the preposition *by* with percentages and fractions:

By what percentage did turnover grow? / It grew by 5.9%. (five point nine percent) / ...by 3.75%.

(by three point seven five percent) / It went up 2 1/2%. (two and a half percent)

...these results give a misleading picture...

– When information from charts and statistics is not so useful:

The graph gives a false picture. / The statistics may give you the wrong idea.

...a "one-off" profit...

– It means a profit which will not be repeated.

We're currently predicting a slowdown...

– Other ways to predict events:

We're forecasting an improvement. / We're expecting a sharp fall.

...analysts are forecasting an upturn...

– An *upturn* is a recovery. / A *downturn* is a decline.

...we're looking at a growth rate of between 1 and 3 percent...

– *Look at* is an informal alternative expression meaning to expect or to predict:

We're looking at a large increase. / What kind of growth are we looking at next year? / As you can see from the graph,...

As you can see from the graph...

– Referring to visual aids:

This chart clearly shows the dramatic fall in production. / At this point on the graph you can see... / Here you can see...

...sales have increased considerably...

– Alternatives to *considerably*:

a lot / a great deal / substantially

...sales picked up in February...

– Other verbs to describe trends:

Sales recovered. (returned to their original level)

Turnover fell back. (declined)

Sales were up/down on last year. (better/worse than last year)

...sales reached a peak in August...

– We can also say:

Sales reached their high/highest point in August.

– The opposite:

Sales reached their low/lowest point in June.

The closure of our Geneva plant in January accounts for the sharp fall...

– *Account for* means to be the reason for. This is a useful term when talking about facts and figures.

How would you account for the fall in sales?

The appointment of a new Sales Manager accounts for the rapid rise in sales last year.

– Note also *due to*:

The fall is due to the closure of the plant.

...sales have continued to decline...

– Further examples:

Sales have continued to fall.

There has been a further fall/decline in sales.

If you compare this six-month period...

– Note the use of a hyphen (-) in *six-month*. Compare:

a three-month period / a period of three months

...there has been very little change...

– Note the use of the present perfect tense to describe change:

Things haven't changed very much. / Things have hardly changed. / Change has been very slight. / Sales have been steady.

British	American
a one-off profit	*a one-shot/one-time profit*
closure	*closing*

Conversations C

4 Listen and repeat.

Advertising

A What are the most common media used for advertising?

B This pie chart shows us that ads on television and outdoor **billboards** or in magazines are more common than those in newspapers, emails or on radio. The Internet is getting more popular than before.

A Do you think the Internet is a good **channel** for marketing?

B Yes, it is. Look at here. It shows Internet advertising is reaching a larger **audience** because it is not limited by time or space.

Branding

A The sales of this brand have increased largely this year.

B Perfect. What are the **highlights**?

A From this bar chart we can see that brand names are important for customers to choose **household goods**. Our sales of this product increased by 13 percent because of its high quality as well as a popular name.

B Our products enjoy a good prospect.

A That's right. According to the sales data, we are becoming more famous for providing better after-sales services.

B Good service is the key to our success!

Promotional Gifts

A It is an effective **promotion** strategy to **distribute** promotional gifts to customers. For example, some lovely dolls with our **logo**.

B I agree with you. We can design some gifts which are cheap and **unique**.

A That's right.

B Any ideas for the design?

A I think umbrellas, cups, fans, or T-shirts are all very good.

B That's great! We can also design raincoats with our product's ads on. In rainy days, the ads are quite **eye-catching**.

Online Promotion

A From the overview we can see how important e-business is becoming nowadays.

B Yes, online promotion accounts for a crucial part of e-business, but the cost is a little bit high.

A It depends. Look at here, the chart says **banners** may cost a lot, but some other promotional ways are not so expensive, for instance, email **newsletters**, online **press releases**, etc.

B It means we can choose some of them according to our budget.

A That's right.

B What is essential for e-business?

A I think **repetition** is the key, and a well-designed website is the **cornerstone**. I suggest that our website should be designed to attract more consumers to click and browse the webpages of our products.

MY GLOSSARY

billboard	*n.*	(尤指路旁的)大型广告牌	unique	*adj.*	独一无二的，与众不同的
channel	*n.*	渠道；方法	eye-catching	*adj.*	引人注目的，抢眼的
audience	*n.*	观众；听众	banner	*n.*	横幅广告，广告条
highlight	*n.*	最精彩的部分	newsletter	*n.*	时事通讯
household goods		家庭用品	press release		新闻稿，通讯稿
promotion	*n.*	促销，推销；宣传	repetition	*n.*	重复
distribute	*v.*	分发，散发；分配	cornerstone	*n.*	基础，基石
logo	*n.*	(公司的)标志，标识			

Useful Expressions

This pie chart shows us that…

– We can also say:

This pie chart illustrates that… / The following bar chart describes that… / The line chart above gives us details about…

Our products enjoy a good prospect.

– We can also say:

Our products have a good prospect. / Our products have a bright future. / The prospect of our products is very bright.

Good service is the key to our success!

– We can also say:

Good service is crucial to our success. / Good service is critical to our success. / Good service is the most important factor for our success.

I agree with you.

– Some examples using *agree*:

I agree with you on this issue.

I agree that he should be invited.

We couldn't agree on what to buy.

They agreed not to tell anyone about what had happened.

...online promotion accounts for a crucial part of e-business...

– *Account for something* means to form the total of something. Some examples using *account for*:

Students account for the vast majority of our customers.

The social services account for a substantial part of public spending.

It should at least account for 50% of the total investment.

I suggest that our website should be designed...

– *I suggest that somebody (should) do* is a way of giving suggestions, for example:

I suggest that we (should) wait a while before we make any firm decisions.

Liz suggested (that) I (should) try the shop on Mill Road.

– Other ways of giving suggestions:

They're advising that children (should) be kept at home.

She demanded that he (should) return the books he borrowed from her.

The rules require that you (should) bring only one guest to the dinner.

British	American
hoarding	*billboard*

Technical Terms

e-business/e-commerce the business of buying and selling goods and services on the Internet, or a particular company that does this 电子商务

budget a plan to show how much money a person or an organisation will earn and how much they will need or be able to spend 预算

Practice

1 Complete each sentence with the correct preposition.

1) First I'd like to talk *about* how we outsource our training.
2) Turnover increased ____________ more than ten percent last year.
3) Sales picked ____________ well in the first quarter of the year.
4) Please bear ____________ me while I find the reference.
5) We're forecasting an increase of ____________ two and three percent.
6) I'd like to finish ____________ thanking you all for your very useful comments.
7) We are forecasting a downturn ____________ the market.
8) Unfortunately, we had to shut ____________ our Geneva plant earlier this year.

2 Write what you would say in these presentation situations. Refer to the Conversations and Useful Expressions.

1) Start a talk. Explain what you are going to talk about.

   Hello everyone. My name's Hiro Rosado and I'd like to talk about…

2) You are giving a presentation and someone asks you to go back to a previous slide. What could you say as you are looking for it?

   ____

   ____

3) Invite questions from the audience.

   ____

   ____

4) Refer to some details on a graph or chart.

   ____

   ____

5) Finish the talk. Thank the audience.

   ____

   ____

3 Match the two parts of the sentences.

1) That leads me to
2) As I mentioned earlier,

a ☐ we hope to finish things soon.
b ☐ to contact me at any time.

3) You are welcome	c	☐	so many of you here.
4) To summarise	d	☐	there are some potential problems.
5) It's good to see	e	☐	what I have said so far…
6) Analysts are forecasting	f	☐	a very healthy outlook for the company.
7) Excuse me	g	*1*	my main point…
8) The graph compares	h	☐	for a moment.
9) Having said that,	i	☐	the number of guests visiting the hotel over a six-month period.

4 Decide if the expressions are up, down or the same.

	Up	Down	The Same
1) Sales have picked up.	☑	☐	☐
2) There has been an increase in sales.	☐	☐	☐
3) Things are slowing down.	☐	☐	☐
4) Turnover jumped last year.	☐	☐	☐
5) It has stayed the same.	☐	☐	☐
6) Overall there has been a decline in the market.	☐	☐	☐
7) The company has recovered.	☐	☐	☐
8) We have seen a rise in turnover.	☐	☐	☐
9) There has been an upturn in the market.	☐	☐	☐
10) We are expecting a downturn.	☐	☐	☐
11) There has been little change.	☐	☐	☐
12) Sales have been steady during the year.	☐	☐	☐

5 Complete the sentences with words used in the Conversations and Useful Expressions.

1) I'm not the best ___*person*___ to answer that question.
2) I didn't catch your ____________. Could you repeat it?
3) Unfortunately the downward ____________ is going to continue.
4) I'd like to make another ____________.
5) The results give a misleading ____________ of last year's performance.
6) What kind of growth ____________ are we hoping to achieve?
7) We are very disappointed with the sharp ____________ in sales.
8) Sales reached their highest ____________ in the summer.
9) A lot has happened during the previous six-month ____________.

6 Complete the sentences with the verbs from the box. Use each verb once only.

catch	repeat	show	account	take	give	~~cost~~	say	fall	bear

1) I'd like to ask how much the project is going to *cost*.
2) I'm afraid I can't ________. I'll check for you.
3) I'm sorry I didn't ________ the question.
4) Let me ________ it for you.
5) I'm not quite ready. Can you ________ with me?
6) Of course. ________ your time.
7) I think these charts ________ a false picture.
8) Yes, they don't really ________ the recent upturn in the market.
9) By what percentage did turnover ________ last year?
10) By 5 percent. I can't ________ for it.

7 Listen to the recording and match the graphs with the descriptions.

1) The graph shows how sales have increased this year. Sales were very poor at the beginning of the year but they began to pick up in March and reached a peak in December. The outlook is very healthy.
2) This has been a difficult year for the company. As you can see, the chart shows the dramatic fall in production at the beginning of the year. Things began to improve but in June there was a serious fire in our factory and this accounts for the sharp fall in production at that time. The situation hasn't changed very much since then.
3) As you can see, we're looking at a growth rate of between 2 and 5 percent in the three-month period, October to December. We're forecasting that this will be up on last year. We are quite happy with the situation.

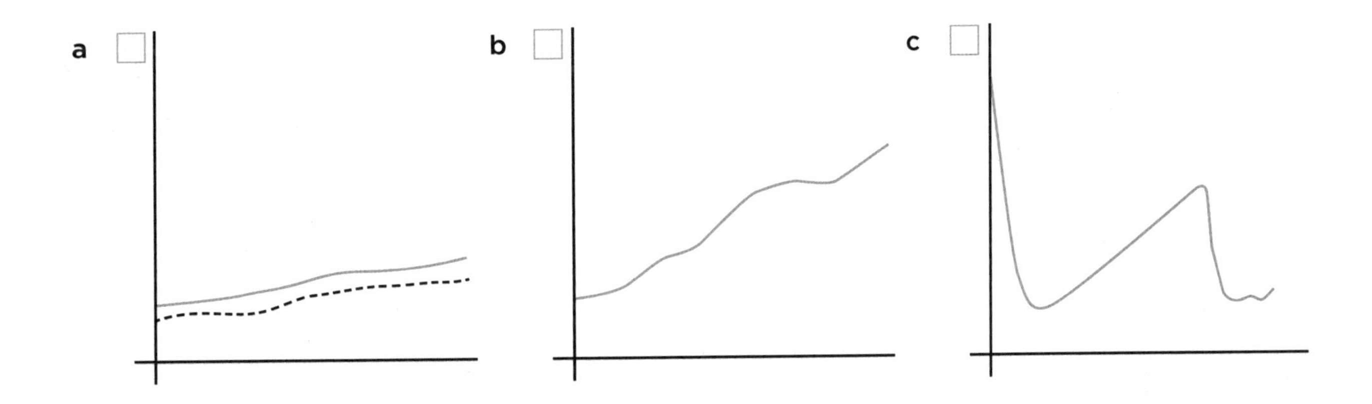

UNIT 5 Meetings

Learning Objectives

Upon completion of the unit, students will be able to:

- set up, postpone or confirm a meeting;
- work through an agenda and reach an agreement in a meeting;
- handle follow-up issues after a meeting.

Starting Off

1 Answer the questions.

1) What type of meetings do you attend most often? Face-to-face or online meetings?

2) Do you prefer to get straight down to business or is it important to start a meeting with small talk?

3) How important is it to have an agenda for meetings?

Conversations A

2 Listen and repeat.

Setting up a Meeting

A Hi, Anna. I'm trying to arrange a meeting for next week. Can you make Tuesday or Thursday afternoon?

B Tuesday would be fine. What time?

A What about 3 o'clock? I don't think we need more than two hours.

B I agree. Is Juan coming, by the way?

A I hope so, but I haven't asked him yet.

Postponing a Meeting

A Hello again. I hope this won't cause you any problems, but I've just spoken to Juan and he can't make Tuesday. Could we make it Thursday instead?

B Just a moment. I'll check my **calendar**. Right, I've got another meeting on Thursday but it should be finished by 3:15. Could we meet at 3:30 **just in case** the meeting **overruns**?

A Of course. I know Juan will be pleased because he didn't want to miss the meeting.

B Fine. See you on Thursday afternoon. I'll send you my **draft proposal** by Monday midday.

A Thanks Anna. Bye.

Setting up a Meeting (a voicemail message)

A I'm sorry I can't take your call at the moment. Please leave your message after the tone and I'll get back to you as soon as I can.

B Hello, Margaret, it's Dagmar here. I'd like to come over to Poznan next week to see you and Alex. There are some things we need to discuss **relating to** the arrangements for the conference. Any day next week except Friday would **suit** me. Could you check with Alex and get back to me? I think we'll need about three hours. Look forward to hearing from you.

Confirming a Meeting by Email

Hi Dagmar,

I've spoken to Alex and the best day for us is Wednesday. I've **booked** the conference room in our office and I'll **order** lunch near our office. Let me know if you would like us to arrange anything special for you. Otherwise I'll see you in the office at 12:30.

Regards,

Margaret

MY GLOSSARY

postpone	*v.*	推迟，使延期	relate to		关于，涉及
calendar	*n.*	日历	suit	*v.*	适合，适宜
just in case		以防万一	confirm	*v.*	确认，确定（安排或会议）
overrun	*v.*	超时；超支	book	*v.*	预订，预约
draft	*adj.*	草拟的，草稿的	order	*v.*	（尤指在饭店或商店）点（饭菜）；订购
proposal	*n.*	提议，建议；计划			

Useful Expressions

I'm trying to arrange a meeting for...

– Note the use of *for*:

...for next month. / ...for next year. / ...for the project group.

Can you make Tuesday?

– This means *Can you come on Tuesday?* Note the different uses of *make*:

Could we make it Thursday instead? / I could make it at 2 p.m. / I can't make the meeting.

Is Juan coming, by the way?

– Use *by the way* to ask for additional information:

By the way, is anyone else coming? / Who else is coming, by the way?

– We can also use *happen to*:

Do you happen to know if Juan is coming?

...it should be finished by 3:15.

– Note that times can be said in two ways:

3:15 (a quarter past three or three fifteen)

3:20 (twenty past three or three twenty)

3:30 (half past three or three thirty)

3:45 (a quarter to four or three forty-five)

By 3:15 means that it could finish earlier than this time.

– Compare:

at 3 o'clock (exactly 3 o'clock)

at around 3 o'clock (maybe a little earlier or later than 3 o'clock)

– Note that *half three* in informal British English is 3:30.

...just in case the meeting overruns.

– Another way of saying:

Just in case it doesn't finish on time.

...he didn't want to miss the meeting.

– Note that *miss* has two meanings:

Unfortunately I had to miss the meeting. / I'm sorry I missed you earlier.

– Compare with:

Juan is a very important member of the team—we really miss him when he is away.

I'd like to come over to Poznan next week...

– *Come over* means to travel from one place to another:

I'm thinking of coming over to visit.

You must come over and see the office.

Any day next week except Friday would suit me.

– *Any day* leaves the options open. The writer could have said:

I'm free every day next week except Friday.

That suits me means *That's a good time for me.*

Could you check with Alex and get back to me?

– *Get back to me* leaves the method of communication open; the contact could be by phone, email or letter.

...I'll order some lunch near our office...

– Some other useful expressions:

Would you prefer to eat out? / Is there anything you don't eat? / Are you a vegetarian? / We can have a working lunch. / We often do business over lunch.

Otherwise I'll see you in the office at 12:30.

– In this example, *otherwise* means *if I don't hear from you*.

British	**American**
Differences in time:	
a quarter past three or three fifteen	*also: a quarter after three*
a quarter to four or three forty-five	*also: a quarter of four*
Differences in dates:	
1/11/03=1 November 2003 (the first of November, two thousand and three)	1/11/03=January 11, 2003 (January eleventh, two thousand three)

Conversations B

3 Listen and repeat.

Working Through an Agenda

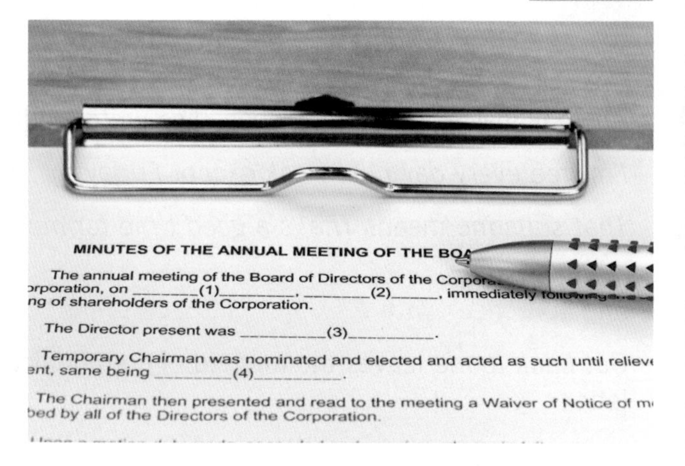

A Has everyone got a copy of the agenda? Lee, could you take the minutes, please?

B No problem.

A Thanks. So, let's start. As we're rather short of time today, I'd like to leave item four until the next meeting. Is that OK with everyone?

B That's fine with me.

A Good, so can we look at item one? That's John's proposal that future department team meetings should be **held** away from the office. What are your thoughts on this?

Reporting Back to a Meeting

A John, could you give us your report?

B Certainly. As you know, I was asked to find out what the people in my department thought about arranging more meetings away from the office. I found that most of my staff **were opposed to** the idea. The **majority** feeling was that they would **prefer to** organise meetings in this building.

A That's interesting. Sandra, what did you find out?

C Quite the **opposite**. In my department, of the fifty people I asked, only five did not like the idea of having meetings away from the office.

Reaching an Agreement

A I think we should **abandon** the idea altogether, does everyone agree?

B Not really. I think we need a **questionnaire** to all the staff so we can find out exactly what they think.

C Is that really necessary? You've heard what John and Sandra have said – there are so many different views. It's not worth it.

A I **suppose** you're right. It just seemed like a good idea to me at the time.

B It is a good idea. Perhaps we could look at it again next year!

Making a Point

A The other point I want to make is that we need to be **informed** about the dates of meetings well **in advance**. I was told about the date of this meeting very late and that caused me a lot of problems.

Some people were not able to come at all. We really must avoid this in the future. Communication is very bad in this company.

B That's not true. Some people don't check their calendars. The date was set three weeks ago and everyone was sent an **invitation**.

MY GLOSSARY

hold	*v.*	召开，举行
be opposed to		反对，不赞成
majority	*n.*	大多数，大部分
prefer to		宁可；更喜欢
opposite	*adj.*	迥异的，截然相反的
reach an agreement		取得一致意见，达成共识
abandon	*v.*	放弃；中止
questionnaire	*n.*	问卷；情况调查表
suppose	*v.*	认为；猜想
make a point		阐明观点；表明看法
inform	*v.*	通知，告知
in advance		预先，事先，提前
invitation	*n.*	邀请函；邀请，约请

Useful Expressions

...I'd like to leave item four until the next meeting.

– We usually talk about *items* or *points* on an agenda.

Can we look at item one?

– Note that we can look at an item on the agenda. Some other useful verbs and prepositions:

Let's move on to item two on the agenda. / Can we go through the minutes? / We need to vote on it.

What are your thoughts on this?

– Asking for opinions:

How do you feel about this? / What do you think? / I'd like to hear everyone's opinion.

...I was asked to find out what the people in my department thought...

– Reporting back:

It was my job to find out about... / You asked me to find out about... / I've talked to the office staff and the general opinion is...

The majority feeling was...

– Majority opinions:

Most people are in favour of the change. / The majority opinion is in favour.

– Minority opinions:

Not many people agree with the idea. / The minority opinion is against it.

...of the fifty people I asked, only five...

– More numbers and percentages:

One in fifty agreed with the idea.

Two in three are against it

Nearly 100 percent of the staff replied to the questionnaire.

A quarter/Half/Three quarters of the staff were in favour.

...does everyone agree?

– Ways to find out if there is agreement:

Are we all in agreement? / Do you have the same opinion? / Does anyone disagree?

Is that really necessary?

– *Really* is used more in spoken English to emphasise what you are saying:

Are you really sure? / Is he really leaving the company? / They really don't want to leave the office.

I suppose you're right.

– The speaker uses *suppose* to admit that the other speaker is, in fact, right.

The other point I want to make...

– Some alternative expressions:

I'd like to make another point. / Just one other point... / I'd like to make one final point.

We really must avoid this in the future.

– Making a strong statement:

It's vital that we avoid this in the future. / It's essential that we make changes. / It's crucial that people should read their messages.

That's not true.

– Note that this is a very direct statement and could be considered impolite. Less direct alternatives:

I'm sorry, but I don't agree. / I don't think that's true. / I'm not sure that's true. / Is that really true?

British	American
favour	*favor*
emphasise	*emphasize*

Conversations C

4 Listen and repeat.

A Follow-up Phone Call (1)

A Hi Kitty. I'm just phoning to let you know what happened in the meeting.

B Thanks. So how did it go?

A Bad news I'm afraid. They **rejected** all of our proposals to change suppliers to AKK. Some of the managers agreed that we needed to change but Anton Trofimov **persuaded** them to leave things as they are.

B So what reasons did he give?

A Anton said he thought that the current arrangements were good enough and finally everyone else agreed with him.

B I don't believe it. How can they be so **short-sighted**?

A Follow-up Phone Call (2)

A Hello again, Kitty. I thought I should let you know immediately that Anton has been having second thoughts. He's been through the figures which I **presented** at the meeting again and he now thinks we've made a good case for moving our business over to AKK.

B Do you want me to do anything?

A No, but thanks for offering. Anton would like me to provide some more information about AKK at another meeting to be held next week. I'll call you tomorrow so we can discuss details then.

B Fine. Speak to you then.

Action Points

Here are the main points covered during the meeting on February 14th and action to be taken.

- Jaroslav to produce a questionnaire to find out how the staff would like to spend the New Year **bonus**.
- Simona to research costs for proposed building project.
- Winston to **look into improving** our **security** systems.
- Tree planting project—no decision made. Leave until the next meeting. The next meeting will be on March 3rd.

Sending Minutes by Email

Ahmed,

I've **attached** the draft minutes of the meeting. Could you **look through** them and check if I have left anything out.

Many thanks.

Manuela

MY GLOSSARY

follow-up	*adj.*	后续的	bonus	*n.*	奖金；红利
reject	*v.*	拒绝接受；拒收	look into		调查，研究
persuade	*v.*	劝服，说服	improve	*v.*	改进，改善
short-sighted	*adj.*	目光短浅的，没有远见的	security	*n.*	保护（措施）；安全（保障）
present	*v.*	提交；展现	attach	*v.*	把……作为电子邮件的附件
action point		行动方案	look through		浏览，快速看

Useful Expressions

I'm just phoning to let you know...

– Announcing the reason for a call:

I'm just phoning to say thank you for doing the minutes. / I'm just calling to remind you about next week's meeting.

Bad news I'm afraid.

– The speaker says *bad news* at the beginning of the sentence for emphasis. He could also have said:

I'm afraid I have some bad news.

– Other examples:

Good news, I'm happy to say. / I'm happy to say I have some good news.

...what reasons did he give?

– Note the use of *give*:

to give a reason / to give an explanation

...short-sighted.

– When you only think about the present, not the future, you are *short-sighted*.

I thought I should let you know immediately...

– You can also say *I wanted to* instead of *I thought* in this situation:

I wanted to let you know what happened.

...Anton has been having second thoughts.

– *Have second thoughts* means to change your opinion after you have thought about it again.

Are you having second thoughts? / On second thoughts, I'd like to accept the proposal.

...he now thinks we've made a good case...

– The speaker uses the word *now* to show that he has changed his mind.

I'll call you tomorrow so we can discuss details then.

– *I will call* is usually reduced to *I'll call* in spoken English. It implies a promise / a firm arrangement:

I'll let you know. / I'll send you a message. / I'll organise it.

Here are the main points...

– We can start the memo with *Here are...*or simply use the following:

The main points. / Action points.

Jaroslav to produce a questionnaire...

– Note the use of infinitive *to* in these statements. This is very common when writing informal action points from a meeting:

Juliet to research costs for the proposed building project.

Winston to look into improving our security systems.

...for proposed building project.

– Note how the article *the* (for the proposed project) can be left out when the memo is in note form.

...no decision made.

– Auxiliary verbs (*was* in this example) can be left out when you write/speak in note form.

I've attached the draft minutes of the meeting.

– Drafts can be first drafts, rough drafts or final drafts. Alternatives:

The draft minutes are attached. / Herewith the draft minutes. (more formal)

...check if I have left anything out.

– Other possibilities:

Let me know if I have forgotten anything. / Check if I have made any mistakes.

British	American
On second thoughts...	*On second thought...*

Technical Terms

agenda a list of matters to be discussed at a meeting 议事日程；（会议的）议程

the minutes the written record of what was said at a meeting 备忘录；会议记录

questionnaire a list of questions that several people are asked so that information can be collected about something 问卷；情况调查表

supplier a company, person, etc. that provides things that people want or need, especially over a long period of time 供应商，提供者

cost the amount of money needed to buy, do, or make something 价格；费用；成本

Practice

1 Complete the sentences with the verbs from the box. Use each verb once only.

~~arrange~~	cover	miss	cause	make	give	report	happen	leave	abandon

1) I'd like to *arrange* a meeting for next week.
2) Can you __________ the meeting on Tuesday?
3) I hope that the changed time won't __________ any problems.
4) I must hurry. I don't want to __________ the meeting.
5) Do you __________ to know if Motoko is going to be there?
6) I don't like it at all. We should __________ the idea.
7) Let's __________ discussion on this point until the next meeting.
8) I'll talk to the staff and __________ back to you next week.
9) Did Tonya __________ a reason why she shouldn't attend?
10) We have a lot of things to __________ in this meeting.

2 Complete the sentences with words used in the Conversations. The first letter of each word is provided.

1) The m*ajority* of the staff were in favour.
2) Can we look at the first i__________ on the agenda?
3) Is it n__________ to send an agenda beforehand?
4) I'd like to leave point two u__________ the next meeting.
5) Can we go t__________ the report now?
6) I can meet any day next week e__________ Monday.
7) Does Tuesday s__________ you?
8) Have we received the results of the q__________ yet?

3 Underline the correct item to complete each sentence.

1) I'm phoning to *let* /*explain* you know what happened.
2) Who is going to *make/take* the minutes?
3) Could you *tell/say* us when you know the answer?
4) I'd like to *make/remind* a point.
5) We need to *take/set* a date for the meeting.
6) We *made/took* a good case for changing the system.

7) Are you *having/taking* second thoughts about the proposal?

8) All of our proposal were *disagreed/rejected*.

4 Complete each sentence with the correct preposition.

1) The meeting should be finished ___*by*___ 3 p.m.

2) I booked the room ________ 1 p.m.

3) I'll see you ________ Thursday at 11 o'clock.

4) I'd like to hear everyone's thoughts ________ the proposal.

5) ________ the ten people I asked, only one was against the idea.

6) It seems like a good idea ________ me.

7) Can we move ________ to the next item ________ the agenda?

8) Most of the participants were ________ favour of the suggestion.

9) One ________ twenty of the staff are unhappy with working conditions.

10) Could you look ________ the minutes and let me know if I've forgotten anything.

11) I hope I haven't left anything ________.

12) Just ________ case I don't see you later, let me give you the papers now.

5 Write what you would say in these situations. Refer to the Conversations and Useful Expressions.

1) Check that everyone has a copy of the agenda.

   Has everybody got a copy of the agenda?

2) Suggest leaving the next item on the agenda until the next meeting.

   I'd like ____.

3) Ask if everyone agrees that date of the next meeting should be changed.

   Does everyone ____?

4) Ask Fiona if she is going to attend the next meeting.

   Are you ____?

5) Call a colleague to tell him/her what happened in the meeting.

   I'm just phoning ____.

6) Tell a colleague that you are sending the agenda as an email attachment.

   I've ____.

7) Say that you have one more point to make.

   Just ____.

8) Ask what people think about the idea.

   What ____?

6 Match the two parts of the sentences.

1) I'd like to leave point three
2) The majority feeling
3) You've all heard
4) Very few people
5) Bad news
6) I'll call you tomorrow
7) Could you check the dates
8) If I don't hear from you
9) Any day except Thursday
10) I graduated

a ☐ are in favour of the changes.
b ☐ and we can discuss details then.
c ☐ is that people want to work shorter hours.
d ☐ I'll expect to see you at 2 p.m.
e ☐ what Maria has said about this.
f ☐ with a degree in Business Administration.
g *1* until the next meeting.
h ☐ suits me.
i ☐ I'm afraid.
j ☐ and get back to me?

7 Complete the sentences with the correct form of the verbs in brackets. Refer to the Conversations and Useful Expressions.

1) Hi, John. *I'm trying* (try) to arrange a meeting for next week.
2) I hope it __________ (not cause) you any problems if we postpone the meeting.
3) I __________ (order) some sandwiches for lunch.
4) I'm sorry I __________ (miss) the last meeting.
5) I __________ (see) you in the conference room at 3 p.m.
6) __________ (everyone/agree) with the proposal? Good, then let's move on.
7) Hello, Anton. I __________ (call) to let you know what happened in the meeting.
8) I don't think that Margaret __________ (read) the report.
9) Memo: Frieda __________ (find out) about tree planting costs.
10) I __________ (attach) the minutes from the last meeting.
11) I __________ (have) second thoughts about your proposals.
12) Everyone __________ (send) a meeting invitation two weeks ago.

8 Listen to the speaker summarising a meeting. Write down the action points.

Marisa *to produce* __________ Michela __________

__________ __________

Bill __________ Satu __________

__________ __________

UNIT 6 Entertaining and Socialising

Learning Objectives

Upon completion of the unit, students will be able to:

- order a meal and pay the bill;
- choose topics of conversation;
- receive and see off customers or clients.

Starting Off

1 Answer the questions.

1) If friends or business contacts visit you, where do you like to entertain them in your local area?
2) How important is it for you to get to know your university contacts socially?
3) Which social topics do you like to discuss? Which topics do you avoid?

Conversations A

2 Listen and repeat.

Coffee or Tea?

A Would you like some coffee?
B Do you have any tea?
A Yes, we do. Do you take milk and sugar?
B No, thanks.

C Can I have a **soft drink**, please?

A Yes, of course. We have some orange juice and some **sparkling water**.

C I'll have an orange juice, please.

Translating the Menu

A I hope you like Russian food. Let me translate the menu for you. I recommend the set menu which is "**borsch**"—that's **beetroot** soup, followed by "buglama", which is a kind of **lamb stew** cooked in **spices**—it **comes with mashed potato** and salad.

B Sounds good. What about **dessert**?

A There's a choice of ice cream.

B I'm happy with that. Let's order.

Ordering a Meal (1)

A We're ready to order. To start, I'd like chicken soup and my colleague would like the **grilled sardines**.

B Thank you. And for your **main course**?

A I'd like fried chicken and French fries and, was it **roast duck** and boiled rice?

C That's right. With a green side salad, please.

B Thank you. And to drink?

A We'd like a bottle of sparkling water, please?

Ordering a Meal (2)

A Are you ready to order?

B Yes, please. I'd like the **steak**, please.

A How would you like it cooked?

B **Medium rare**.

A Thank you. Are you having a **starter**?

B No, thanks. I don't have much time.

Paying the Bill

A That was very good. Can we have the bill, please?

B Here you are, sir.

A Excuse me, but could you tell me what this is for?

B It's for the bread.

A Oh yes, I see. Do you take credit cards?

B I'm sorry, we don't. If you need some cash, there's a cash machine just across the road.

MY GLOSSARY

soft drink		不含酒精的饮料；汽水	dessert	*n.*	餐后甜点
sparkling water		气泡水；苏打水	grilled sardine		烤沙丁鱼
borsch	*n.*	罗宋汤（俄罗斯甜菜浓汤）	main course		主菜
beetroot	*n.*	甜菜根	roast duck		烤鸭
lamb stew		炖羊肉	steak	*n.*	（尤指）牛排
spice	*n.*	香料；调味品	medium rare		三分熟
come with		与……一起供给	starter	*n.*	（一餐的）开胃品，头盘
mashed potato		土豆泥			

Useful Expressions

Would you like some coffee?

– You can also ask if someone would like a drink or snack by using the word with rising intonation:

More coffee? Tea? Sugar? Milk?

Do you take milk and sugar?

– Also note:

How do you like your coffee? / Just a little milk, please. / Help yourself to milk and sugar. / No milk for me, thanks.

Can I have a soft drink, please?

– Soft drinks are non-alcoholic drinks:

fruit juices, include orange juice, apple juice and grapefruit juice

I'd prefer water. / Would you like sparkling or still water?

Let me translate the menu for you.

– When you need a translation:

Could you translate the menu? / What's that in Italian? / Do you have an English menu?

..."borsch"—that's beetroot soup,...

– Language for explaining the menu:

It's a speciality of this region. / Would you like to try one of the specials? / It's a kind of soup. / It tastes like chicken. / It's delicious. I recommend it.

We're ready to order.

– Or the waiter/waitress can say:

Are you ready to order? / Can I take your order?

And for your main course?

– Stages of a meal:

I don't really want a starter. / Can I see the dessert menu? / Thank you. That was very good.

I'd like fried chicken...

– Some methods of cooking:

roast (roast duck, roast beef) / boiled (boiled rice, boiled potatoes) / steamed (steamed vegetables, steamed fish) / grilled (grilled sardines)

Medium rare.

– Other ways of cooking steak:

rare, medium, well done

Can we have the bill, please?

– The waiter might ask:

Would you like anything else?

– Possible replies:

No, just the bill, please. / Another coffee, please.

Excuse me, but could you tell me what this is for?

– Asking about the bill:

Sorry, I don't understand the bill. / Is service included? / We ordered one salad but you've charged us for two.

Do you take credit cards?

– Other useful expressions:

Can I pay by card? / How much do you normally tip? (not a question we usually ask the waiter!)

...there's a cash machine just across the road.

– *A cash machine, cash dispenser or cash point* (UK) = an ATM (Automatic Teller Machine) (US)

British	American
Do you take milk and sugar?	*Do you use milk and sugar?*
beetroot soup	*beet soup*
mashed potato	*mashed potatoes*
Can I have the bill, please?	*Can I have the check, please?*
a starter	*an appetizer*
Is service included?	*Is the gratuity included?*

Conversations B

3 Listen and repeat.

Where You Live

A Where do you live, Xavier?

B In Sitges, near Barcelona.

A Oh, I know Barcelona very well. It's one of my favourite cities.

B And mine. Sitges is a beautiful little town just along the coast from Barcelona. I've lived there all my life. It's a great place for a holiday but best to go **out of season**.

Starting a Conversation

A Did you see the football match last night?

B Yes, I did. I thought Pogba played very well.

A So did I. I thought his first goal was **fantastic**. So you like football, do you?

B I quite like it. I watch international matches and I follow my local team, but I prefer basketball.

Family Matters

A Where are you going for your summer holiday?

B I'm going to the French Alps with the family. We all want to do different things, so it's a great place for us. My son and daughter can go **mountain biking**, and my partner and I can go walking and play some golf.

A How old are your children?

B Eleven and thirteen. What about you? Do you have any children?

A Yes, but they're all grown up. They don't want to come on holiday with us any more.

Cultural Advice

A I've been invited to dinner with Paulo and Maria this evening but I don't know what to wear. I'd also like to take a small present. Do you have any suggestions?

B Just be **casual**. I'm sure they'd **appreciate** some flowers and maybe something from Scotland.

A I've got a box of Scottish **biscuits** with me.

B That would be fine.

Sensitive Issues

A I'm looking forward to meeting David this afternoon.

B Oh, haven't you heard? He's left the company.

A I'm sorry to hear that. What happened? I thought he was doing very well with you.

B He was, but there were a few problems. I'm afraid I can't really **go into** it now.

A I understand. Tell me another time.

MY GLOSSARY

out of season		在淡季	biscuit	*n.*	饼干
fantastic	*adj.*	极好的，极出色的	sensitive	*adj.*	敏感的
mountain biking		山地自行车运动	issue	*n.*	问题
casual	*adj.*	（衣服）休闲的；便装的	go into		详述，详谈
appreciate	*v.*	欣赏，赏识；感激			

Useful Expressions

Where do you live, Xavier?

– Note how English speakers often use a person's first name to be friendly and engaging. Note, however, that this is not appropriate in all cultures.

Oh, I know Barcelona very well.

– A typical response for keeping a conversation going. Some other possibilities:

Oh, I've been there. / Really? What's it like? / Lucky you! / That's a nice place to live.

It's a great place for a holiday...

– Some other ways of recommending (and not recommending) somewhere for a holiday:

I always spend my summer holidays there. / You must go there. / I wouldn't recommend it. / It isn't a good place for a holiday.

Did you see the football match last night?

– Not everyone likes football! Some other ways to start a conversation:

How was the weather when you left home? / Have you seen any good films recently? / Have you bought any souvenirs?

So you like football, do you?

– Note the use of the question tag for engaging the other speaker:

Terrible weather, isn't it? / You're working next week, aren't you? / Liz is coming this evening, isn't she?

Where are you going for your summer holiday?

– Some ways of keeping the conversation going:

Do you travel a lot on business? / What are you doing at the weekend? / What are your first impressions of the town?

My son and daughter can go mountain biking,...

– Note some verbs which go with sports:

go biking/swimming/riding

play tennis/golf/football

do gymnastics/weightlifting

Do you have any children?

– Talking about your relatives:

My uncle/aunt worked for the company.

My niece/nephew lives in Canada.

My cousin is getting married next year.

...I don't know what to wear.

– Some advice:

It's very informal. / Wear something casual. / You'll need to wear a collar and tie. / What you're wearing is fine.

I'm sure they'd appreciate some flowers...

– *They'd appreciate*...means *they would really like*...

I'm sorry to hear that.

– Other possible responses:

Really? / That's a shame! / I don't believe it!

...I can't really go into it now.

– When you would prefer not to say anything:

Sorry, but I don't really want to talk about it. / Do you mind if I tell you later? / Can we talk about it later?

I understand.

– A useful response to demonstrate that the speaker is happy to be told the news another time. Alternatively:

No problem!

British	**American**
football match	*soccer game*
summer holiday	*summer vacation*
a box of biscuits	*a package of cookies*
You'll need to wear a collar and tie.	*You'll need to wear shirt and tie.*

Conversations C

4 Listen and repeat.

Shopping

A I wonder if it is possible to arrange shopping for us?

B Certainly. Is there anything you want to buy particularly?

A I'd like to buy some British **specialties**. It is said that the discount before Christmas is very big.

B For British specialties, I recommend Fortnum & Mason, an old royal food department store. I'm sure you can buy what you want there.

A Sounds good.

At **Fortnum & Mason**

B Do you find anything you like?

A Look! The packing of the tea is **exquisite**. It is said that British people are very fond of drinking tea. The tea here should be very good.

B You are right. British people like to drink English afternoon tea. After **brewing**, the taste of English tea becomes very unique. Tea is not only light, but also cheap, which can be a good gift.

A Ok, I'll buy some tea. I've heard that chocolates in England are really good, too. Do you have any here?

B Of course, there are many kinds of **delectable handmade** English chocolates. Which one do you prefer?

A I have difficulty choosing among them. Can you give me some advice?

B I recommend these **selection** boxes which contain a **multitude** of **deliciousness**, from mixed milk & dark chocolate selection boxes to our ever popular rose & **violet** creams.

A Great, I'll take this milk & dark chocolate selection box.

Going **Sightseeing**

A Good morning. Since we have finished our work, why don't we go and visit some interesting places?

B Good idea. That's exactly what I am thinking about.

A Is there anywhere you want to go particularly?

B Could you show me some **scenic spots** with local **characteristics**?

A It would be a pity to come all the way to London but not visit the Big Ben.

B That's a good idea. Let's go now.

Giving Gifts

A As your visit is **coming to an end**, we'd like to give you a **souvenir** as a present.

B Oh, thank you. That's very nice of you.

A We know you are very fond of tea, so we would like to present you with English black tea. I hope you like it.

B Wow, great, I enjoy it very much. Thank you so much.

A We're glad you like it. By the way, we have prepared some small gifts for your colleagues in your office.

B They will love it. You are so kind!

A It's my pleasure.

Farewell

A It's very kind of you to come and **see me off**.

B It's my pleasure.

A Thank you for your **hospitality**. I've had a very pleasant experience here these days. I hope you can come to our company when you are free.

B Thank you for your invitation. I hope to visit your company soon. Have a nice trip.

A Thank you.

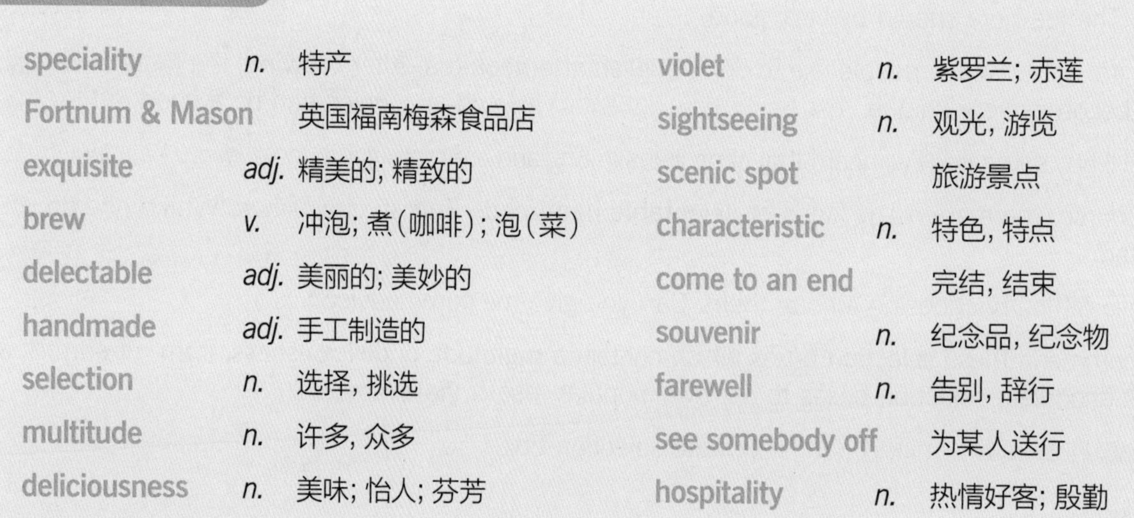

MY GLOSSARY

speciality	n.	特产
Fortnum & Mason		英国福南梅森食品店
exquisite	adj.	精美的; 精致的
brew	v.	冲泡; 煮(咖啡); 泡(菜)
delectable	adj.	美丽的; 美妙的
handmade	adj.	手工制造的
selection	n.	选择, 挑选
multitude	n.	许多, 众多
deliciousness	n.	美味; 怡人; 芬芳
violet	n.	紫罗兰; 赤莲
sightseeing	n.	观光, 游览
scenic spot		旅游景点
characteristic	n.	特色, 特点
come to an end		完结, 结束
souvenir	n.	纪念品, 纪念物
farewell	n.	告别, 辞行
see somebody off		为某人送行
hospitality	n.	热情好客; 殷勤

Useful Expressions

I wonder if it is possible to arrange shopping for us?

– *Wonder* is used at the beginning of a request to make it more formal and polite:

I wonder whether you could pass me the butter?

I wonder what the future holds for you and me.

Tea is not only light, but also cheap...

– *Not only...(but) also* is used to say that two related things are true or happen, especially when this is surprising or shocking:

Not only did he turn up late, he also forgot his books.

If this project fails, it will affect not only our department, but also the whole organisation.

Do you have any here?

– Other useful expressions:

Do you have any for sale? / Do you have any to sell...

...why don't we go and visit some interesting places?

– *Why don't/not* is used to make a suggestion or to express an agreement:

Why not use my car? You'll fit more in.

Why don't you come with us?

It would be a pity to come all the way to London and not visit the Big Ben.

– *Would* is used to refer to a situation that you believed, hoped or expected to happen:

I would hate to miss the show.

I'd go myself, but I'm too busy.

That's very nice of you.

– Some alternative expressions:

It's very kind of you. / You are so kind.

It's very kind of you to come and see me off.

– Note the use of *It's very kind of you...:*

It's very kind of you to help us. / It's very kind of you to come all the way to meet me.

British	American
shop	*store*
supermarket	*grocery store*
chips	*French fries*
toilet	*bathroom*
sweet	*candy*

Technical Terms

contact a person, especially someone in a high position, who can usually give you information that will help you at work or socially （尤指身居高位，能提供有用信息或意见的）熟人，（社会）关系

bill a request for payment of money owed, or the piece of paper on which it is written 账单

credit card a small plastic card that can be used as a method of payment, the money being taken from you at a later time 信用卡

cash money in the form of notes and coins, rather than cheques or credit cards 现金，现款

discount a reduction in the usual price 减价，打折

Practice

1 Write what you would say in these situations. Refer to the Conversations and Useful Expressions.

1) Tell the waiter/waitress that you would like to order your meal.

We're ready to order. / We'd like to order.

2) You don't understand the menu written in Turkish. Ask a colleague for help.

____

3) Order something to eat in a restaurant.

____

4) Ask for the bill.

____

5) Check an item on the bill that you do not understand.

____

6) Ask a business acquaintance where he/she lives.

____

7) Say something about where you live.

____

8) Say something about your holiday plans for the year.

____

9) You hear that a business contact has left the company. What do you say?

____

2 Complete each sentence with the correct preposition.

1) How do you say that ___*in*___ English?
2) What would you like ________ your main course?
3) The grilled chicken comes ________ fried potatoes.
4) Help yourselves ________ salad.
5) Can I pay ________ credit card?
6) Sydney is a great place ________ a holiday.
7) Where are you going ________ holiday this year?
8) I can't really go ________ detail now.
9) Can we talk ________ it later?

3 Complete the dialogue with the expressions a–h.

a I wasn't surprised
b So, what's happening at work
c I thought she really enjoyed her job
d Fine, thanks
e Sarah is leaving the company next month
f Yes, I heard that
g How are things
h Really

A Hi Nigel. (1) ____________________?
B (2) ____________________. (3) ____________________?
A Some sad news I'm afraid. (4) ____________________.
B (5) ____________________.
A I couldn't believe it. (6) ____________________.
B (7) ____________________? (8) ____________________.

4 Complete the phrases 1)–8) with the verbs in the box and match them with a–h to make questions.

accept	wear	~~have~~	take	see	happened	watch	know

1) Can I *have*
2) Do you __________ all
3) Do you __________ if there is
4) Do you __________
5) Would anyone like to __________
6) Did you __________
7) What clothes should I __________
8) What has __________

a ☐ to David? Is he OK?
b ☐ the basketball game yesterday?
c ☐ the dessert menu?
d ☐ credit cards?
e ☐ sugar in your coffee?
f ☐ to the reception?
g ☐ a cash machine nearby?
h *1* the chicken and vegetable soup, please?

5 Choose an appropriate response.

1) Do you have any turkey?
2) Do you take sugar?
3) And for your main course?

a ☐ Yes, I did.
b ☐ It's a kind of bread.
c ☐ I understand.

4) Excuse me, what's this for? d [ ] It's a service charge.
5) And what would you like to drink? e [ ] Tea, please.
6) How would you like it cooked? f [1] I'm very sorry, we don't.
7) Did you play golf yesterday? g [ ] I'll have the chicken.
8) I can't really discuss this now. h [ ] Not really.
9) Would you recommend Elohlleh for a holiday? i [ ] I'd like it fried.
10) What's a "tortilla"? j [ ] No, thanks.

6 Which of the following sports and activities go with the verbs *play* and *go*. Look the words up in a dictionary if you do not know them.

walking	golf	climbing	badminton	volleyball	hiking
basketball	diving	snorkelling	tennis	ping pong	cycling	ailing

play	
go	

7 Complete the sentences with the words in the box.

order	appreciate	favourite	sensitive	recommend

1) "What's your ________ colour?""Green."
2) We really ________ all the help you gave us last weekend.
3) I can ________ the chicken in mushroom sauce—it's delicious.
4) "Can I take your ________ now?" asked the waiter.
5) She's very ________ about her weight.

8 Put the conversation in the right order and then listen to the recording to check your answers.

a [ ] What are you going to do while you're there?
b [ ] Why Hereford?
c [ ] It's a beautiful part of the world.
d [1] Where are you going
e [ ] To the UK.
f [ ] and we have some friends who live there.
g [ ] We're staying in a small hotel in Hereford.
h [ ] for your holiday this year?
I [ ] We're planning to do some walking
j [ ] and there are some excellent places to eat
k [ ] Maybe next year.
l [ ] You must go there.

UNIT 7 Travel

Learning Objectives

Upon completion of the unit, students will be able to:

- book a flight or a room in a hotel;
- check in and out at an airport or in a hotel;
- complain about the problems during travel.

Starting Off

1 Answer the questions.

1) Do you often travel for business and pleasure? If so, where do you travel to?
2) How do you prefer to travel and why?
3) Have you had any interesting travel experiences that you would like to share?

Conversations A

2 Listen and repeat.

Checking in for a Flight

A Can I have your ticket and passport, please? Thank you. Would you like an **aisle** or a window seat?

B I'd like an aisle seat if possible.

A OK. I have given you a seat in the **exit row**. Is that all right?

B Yes, that's fine. Thanks. And I'd like to sit next to my colleague if possible.

A I'm sorry. We don't have any more seats together. Could you talk to the **cabin attendant** when you **board** the plane?

Hiring a Car

A Hello, I'd like to book a hire car for three days from March 14th–17th, please. Do I need an international driving licence to drive here?

B No, but there is a **charge** for an extra driver.

A So how much will it cost **in total**?

B $300. How would you like to pay?

A By credit card, please.

Taking the Train

A A **single** to Munich, please.

B First or second class?

A **First class**, please.

B OK. That will be 90 euros. Please sign here.

A Do I need to **reserve** a seat?

B No, the seat reservation is included in the price.

Booking a Hotel

A Wellington Hotel. Can I help you?

B Yes, I've been trying to book a room on your hotel website but I can't complete the booking.

A Sorry, sir. I can do the booking for you.

B Thank you. I'd like to book a twin room for two nights, the 12th and 13th of June.

A Just one moment. I'll check our **availability**. Can I have your name please?

B Yes, it's Cook. I won't be arriving until 11 p.m. Do you need my credit card number to hold the reservation?

A Yes, please.

Checking into a Hotel

A Hello, I have a reservation in the name of Perry.

B I'm sorry, I cannot find a booking in that name. Did you book the room yourself?

A No, my company, Carditis, booked it.

B Ah yes, here it is. Could you fill in this form, please? Would you like a smoking or non-smoking room?

A A non-smoking room, please, with a bath and a balcony if possible.

B We have a non-smoking room with a balcony on the 10th floor. Enjoy your stay.

MY GLOSSARY

check in		办理登机手续；登记入住
aisle	*n.*	（客机、电影院或教堂座席间的）走廊，过道
exit row		紧急出口
cabin	*n.*	（飞机）座舱，机舱
attendant	*n.*	服务员，侍者
board	*v.*	（使）上（船、火车或飞机）
charge	*n.*	（尤指某一活动或服务的）收费，费用，价格
in total		总计
single	*n.*	单程票；单身
first class		（飞机的）头等舱
reserve	*v.*	预定，预留
availability	*n.*	可得性，可用性

Useful Expressions

Would you like an aisle or a window seat?

– Seating preferences:

I'd prefer an aisle seat. / I don't really want a middle seat. / Do you have a seat in the exit row? / I'd like to change my seat.

…I'd like to book a hire car…

– Useful expressions when you need to hire a car:

Is there a charge for an extra driver? / Does it include insurance? / Where do I return the car? / Do you need my driving licence?

How would you like to pay?

– Other expressions for making payments:

How do you want to pay? / Are you paying by cheque/credit/debit card? / I'd prefer to pay in cash.

A single to Munich, please.

– Useful expressions at the ticket office:

I'd like a first class return to London, please. / Which platform do I need? / Is there a restaurant car?

Do I need to reserve a seat?

– More expressions for making reservations:

Do I need to book in advance? / Are seat reservations compulsory? / I'd like a forward/backward-facing seat.

I'd like to book a twin room…

– Some hotel room options:

A double/single room.

A quiet room with a good view. / A suite with a balcony.

An en suite room. (a room with a separate bathroom) / A shared bathroom.

I won't be arriving until 11 p.m.

– Alternatively we can say:

I hope to be there by 11 p.m. / I'm hoping to arrive by 11 p.m. / I should be there by 11 p.m.

…I have a reservation in the name of Perry.

– When you arrive at the hotel, you can say:

My name is (Mr Perry). / Do you have a reservation for a (Mr Perry)? / The reservation was made by my company.

Could you fill in this form, please?

– Some hotels might not ask you to fill in a form:

I just need your passport. / Just sign here, please.

British	**American**
a hire car	*a rental car*
a non-smoking room	*a no-smoking room*
a double/single room	Hotels in the US use varying terminology but these are usual: *a single = room with one double bed* *a double = a room with two double beds* *a queen = a room with one queen size bed* *a king = a room with one king size bed*
an ensuite room	This phrase is not used in American English.
We have a non-smoking room with a balcony on the 10th floor.	Note that the 10th floor in the UK would be the 11th floor in the US.
ground floor	*first floor*
first floor	*second floor*
I just need to see your passport.	Americans usually use their driver's licence or a special ID card for identification.
platform 1	*track 1*
single ticket	*one-way ticket*
return ticket	*round trip*
underground	*subway*

Conversations B

3 Listen and repeat.

At the Check-in Desk

A Can I see your **hand luggage**, please?

B I just have this bag and a **laptop**.

A Could you put them on the **scales**? I'm afraid the bag will have to go in the **hold**.

B Is that really necessary? It's very small.

A I'm afraid so.

A Flight Delay

A I'm sorry Carmen, but I'm not going to get to the meeting on time. There was a delay coming into the airport and I've just missed my **connection**. If I'm lucky, I'll get a seat on the flight that leaves in half an hour.

B Don't worry, as long as you're here for the afternoon session, it doesn't matter too much.

A Thanks. I'll let you know if I don't manage to catch the flight, otherwise expect to see me about 12:30—in time for lunch.

A Tight Connection

A Excuse me. I have a connection to Chicago at 5:00. Am I going to make it?

B Yes, there will be a minibus waiting at the gate to take you to **terminal** B. There shouldn't be a problem.

A What about my luggage? I'm worried that my bags won't make the connection even if I do.

B Don't worry, the minibus will take you and your luggage. There are some other passengers who also have tight connections.

A Thanks for your help. I'll **keep my fingers crossed**.

A Hotel Mix-up

A Hello, Reception.

B Hello, it's Amanda Lin from Room 205. I asked for a non-smoking room but someone has been smoking in this room. Oh yes, and the TV doesn't work. Also there are no drinks in the **minibar** and the bed hasn't been made. I'd like to change rooms.

A I'm very sorry, madam. I'll organise a different room for you and send someone up immediately to help you with your luggage.

A Payment Problem

A I'm sorry but we need some **identification** if you'd like to pay by card.

B Oh, I don't think I have any identification with me and I don't have enough cash. I'm sure I paid by card last time I was here.

A Yes, we do accept credit cards but only if the bill is under 200 euros. I'm afraid it's a security rule.

B I understand. Can I pay 200 euros with my card and the rest in cash?

A Yes, that would be fine

MY GLOSSARY

hand luggage		手提行李
laptop	*n.*	手提电脑，便携式电脑
scale	*n.*	磅秤；天平
hold	*n.*	（轮船或飞机的）货舱
delay	*n.*	延迟，延误，延期
connection		（火车、轮船、飞机等的）联运
terminal	*n.*	站台；候机楼，航空站
keep one's fingers crossed		祈求好运，祈愿，祷告
mix-up	*n.*	差错；失败
minibar	*n.*	迷你吧（酒店客房内的小冰箱）
payment	*n.*	付款，支付
identification	*n.*	身份证明

Useful Expressions

I just have this bag and a laptop.

– *Just* means *only* in this example. Other examples:

I just need five minutes. / I just need to check your visa.

...the bag will have to go in the hold.

– Problems with hand luggage:

It can go under my seat. / Can I put it in the overhead lockers? / It's too large to go in the cabin.

...I'm not going to get to the meeting on time.

– *On time* means happening or done at a particular moment. Compare:

I'll be there in time for lunch. (eary enough before lunch)

I won't be there on time for Petra's talk. (at the exact time before Petra's talk begins)

Let's meet for lunch. I'll call you ahead of time to decide exactly when and where. (earlier than a particular moment)

...I've just missed my connection.

– Catching another flight:

When's the next flight? / Where is the check-in desk? / How far is it to the gate?

I'll let you know if I don't manage to catch the flight,...

– Notice how we can use *manage*:

I just managed to catch the flight.

I hope you manage with all your luggage—it looks heavy.

Can you manage? Can I help you?

...there will be a minibus waiting at the gate...

– Making sure you catch the flight:

I'm worried I won't make the connection. / Are you sure I'll make it? / You'll have to hurry.

I'll keep my fingers crossed.

– If you want to wish someone else good luck, say:

Fingers crossed! / Good luck!

I asked for a non-smoking room...

– Other complaints:

The TV doesn't work. / The air-conditioning doesn't work. / It's very smoky in the room. / The room is very dusty/dirty/noisy.

...the bed hasn't been made.

– Note the use of the present perfect passive:

The room hasn't been cleaned.

The bins haven't been emptied.

– Compare with the past simple passive:

The room was cleaned this morning.

The bins weren't emptied yesterday.

...we need some identification...

– Some responses:

What kind of identification do you need? / I don't have my passport on me. / I've left my documents behind.

...I don't have enough cash.

– Problems:

I've only got twelve thousand yen. / I've spent all my money. / I'm sorry to ask, but can you lend me some money?

...we do accept credit cards...

– *Do* is used here for emphasis—don't overuse it. We would normally say:

We accept contactless payments.

British	**American**
the hold	*the cargo compartment*
overhead lockers	*overhead bins*
The bins haven't been emptied.	*The wastebaskets haven't been emptied.*
I've left my documents behind.	*I left my documents behind* (American English usually uses the simple past tense.)
cancelled	*canceled*

Conversations C

4 Listen and repeat.

Booking a Flight

A British Airways. Can I help you?

B Yes. I'd like to book a ticket from New York to Barcelona on May 6th for one person.

A Let me check. I'm afraid that all the flights of that day before 12 o'clock are fully booked. How about the flights in the afternoon? There are seats **available** on a flight leaving at 1 p.m.

B I think it's suitable. I'd like to book a seat on it.

A Sure. May I have your name, please?

B It's Mr Peter Anderson.

A First class or **economy**?

B First class, please.

A OK. Let me confirm your reservation. It is one first class ticket on May 6th at 1 p.m. from New York to Barcelona for Mr Peter Anderson. Is that right?

B That's right.

At the Concierge Desk

A Good morning, the Concierge Desk. Can I help you?

B Yes. I have to **check out** in 25 minutes for something urgent, but I don't know where to put my luggage after I check out.

A Don't worry. We offer service of checking your luggage. May I have your name and room number, please?

B Jimmy Carter, Room 166.

A Mr Carter, I'll send a bellboy to Room 166 to fetch your luggage at once. Please be sure to put your name **tag** on your **suitcases**.

B Is it charged or free?

A It is free for 24 hours.

At the Check-out Desk

A Good afternoon, sir. Can I help you?

B Yes, I'd like to check out.

A OK. Would you please give me your **keycard**?

B Here you are.

A Thank you, sir. The total is 110 euros. How would you like to pay, in cash or by credit card?

B I'd like to pay by credit card. Here you are.

A Thank you, sir. Please sign your name here.

At the Airport Exchange Office

A Can I help you, sir?

B Yes, I'd like to **change** my US dollars into euros.

A The exchange rate today is 82.8 euros to 100 dollars. How much would you like to change, sir?

B 400 dollars. Here you are.

A 400 dollars. The exchange is 331.2 euros. May I see your passport, please?

B Sure. Here you are.

A Please fill in the **exchange memo**. Be careful to fill in your passport number, the total sum, your **permanent** address and sign your name here as well.

MY GLOSSARY

available	adj.	可获得的；可用的	keycard	n.	门卡
economy (class)	n.	（飞机的）经济舱	change	v.	兑换
check out		办理退房手续，结账离开	exchange memo		外币兑换单
tag	n.	标签，标牌	permanent	adj.	固定的；永久的；常在的
suitcase	n.	（旅行用的）手提箱			

Useful Expressions

I'd like to book a ticket from New York to Barcelona on May 6th for one person.

– More language for making reservations for a flight/train/restaurant:

I've booked you on the 10 o'clock flight. / I'd like to book a table for two for 8 o'clock tonight. / I've reserved a room in the name of Jones.

There are seats available on a flight leaving at 1 p.m.

– Some expressions about *available*:

This was the only room available. / Information on travel in New Zealand is available at the hotel. / The leaflet is available free of charge from post offices. / Will she be available this afternoon?

May I have your name, please?

– Other language for asking names:

Would you please tell me your name? / May I ask your name, please?

Let me confirm your reservation.

– It is very important to repeat the customer's booking information such as his/her personal information, date, etc.

We offer service of checking your luggage.

– There are some services provided for customers in hotel reception, such as calling a taxi, renting a car, checking luggage, valet parking, receiving and sending packages and booking tickets.

Is it charged or free?

– *Charge* means to ask an amount of money for goods or a service, for example:

The restaurant charged £20 for dinner.

We won't charge you for delivery.

He only charged me half price.

I'd like to change my US dollars into euros.

– *Change sth (into sth)* means to exchange the money of one country into the money of another country. More examples:

Where can I change dollars into yen?

You can change back unused dollars into pounds at the bank.

British	American
book	*reserve*
luggage	*baggage*
aeroplane	*airplane*
bellboy	*bellhop*

Technical Terms

reception the place in a hotel or office building where people go when they first arrive （旅馆或办公楼的）接待处，服务台，前台

connection a bus, train, plane, etc. that arrives at a time that allows passengers to get on after getting off another one, so that they can continue their journey （供中转旅客换乘的）接驳交通工具（如公车、火车、飞机等）

cabin attendant / flight attendant someone who serves passengers on an aircraft （客机的）乘务员

twin room a room in a hotel for two people with two single beds （旅馆中）有两张单人床的双人房

double room a room in a hotel for two people with one double bed （旅馆中的）双人间，双人房，大床房

concierge someone who is employed in a hotel to help guests arrange things, such as theatre tickets and visits to restaurants （帮助客人安排戏票、餐馆等事宜的）旅馆服务台人员，礼宾员

bellboy a person in a hotel employed to carry suitcases, open doors, etc. for guests （旅馆的）男侍者

exchange rate the rate at which the money of one country can be changed for the money of another country 汇率，兑换率

Practice

1 Complete the sentences with words used in the Conversations and Useful Expressions. Write the words in the grid.

1) Sorry, I wanted a return ticket, not a *single* .
2) I have a __________ in the name of Tiller.
3) I'm keeping my fingers __________ that I'll make my flight connection.
4) We need to see some __________—a passport, a driving licence.
5) If I'm very __________ I'll catch the flight.
6) I thought the room was en suite. I'd prefer not to share a __________.
7) I have a superb room with a south-facing __________
8) I asked for a window seat, not an __________ seat.
9) It took so long to clear passport control that I __________ my flight.

1) S I N G L E

2)

3)

4)

5)

6)

7)

8)

9)

2 Write what you would say in these situations. Refer to the Conversations and Useful Expressions.

1) You are at the flight check-in desk. The check-in assistant insists that your hand luggage needs to go in the hold.

   Is that necessary? It's very light/small, etc.

2) Tell the airline check-in clerk your seating preferences.

   ____

3) Phone a hotel and book a double room.

   ____

4) You arrive at your hotel. What do you say to the receptionist?

   ____

5) Phone a colleague to say that your flight has been delayed.

   ____

6) You have a tight flight connection. Explain your problem to the cabin attendant.

   ____

3 Complete each sentence with the correct preposition.

1) I don't have my passport *on* me.
2) Please fill __________ the registration form.

3) Was the booking made ____________ the name of Kerry?

4) Is there room for your bag ____________ your seat?

5) The flight leaves ____________ half an hour.

6) I'd like to hire a car ____________ a week.

7) If we leave now, we should be there ____________ time.

8) I asked for a room ____________ a bath.

9) Unfortunately, I don't have any identification ____________ me.

4 Match the two parts of the sentences.

1) Someone will help you
2) I don't have enough
3) I'll let you know if
4) I'm worried that
5) I won't be arriving
6) I'm hoping to be there
7) I'd like to pay
8) I would like

a ☐ cash on me.
b ☐ I won't make the connection.
c ☐ by 3 p.m.
d *1* with your luggage.
e ☐ a non-smoking room, please.
f ☐ I manage to catch the flight.
g ☐ until 3 p.m.
h ☐ by credit card.

5 Write alternative expressions. Refer to the Conversations and Useful Expressions.

1) Is it necessary to reserve a seat?

Do I need to reserve a seat?

2) Does the price include a seat reservation?

____

3) I'll arrive at 11 p.m. or later.

____

4) I'd rather pay in cash.

____

5) A car will be waiting for you outside the terminal.

____

6) I'll call you if I don't manage to catch the flight.

____

6 Rewrite these sentences in the passive voice.

1) No one has made the bed.

The bed hasn't been made.

2) No one told me about the flight delay.

____

3) They put my luggage in the hold.

____

4) No one has cleaned the room today.

____

5) Someone has already filled in the form.

____

6) Someone booked the taxi last night.

____

7) They cancelled my flight.

____

8) They gave me a first class ticket.

____

7 Listen to the conversations and complete the gaps.

1) **A** ______________________, please?
   B It's Ahmed Salem.
2) **A** ______________________ for Tuesday night.
   B A single or a double?
3) **A** I hope you ______________________.
   B Thanks. Wish me luck!
4) **A** I've ______________________.
   B When's the next flight?
5) **A** Can I ______________________?
   B Yes, of course.
6) **A** The TV in my room ______________________.
   B I'll send someone to look at it.
7) **A** Can I see your passport, please?
   B Yes, of course. ______________________.
8) **A** Where ______________________?
   B Here, please.

UNIT 8

Written Messages

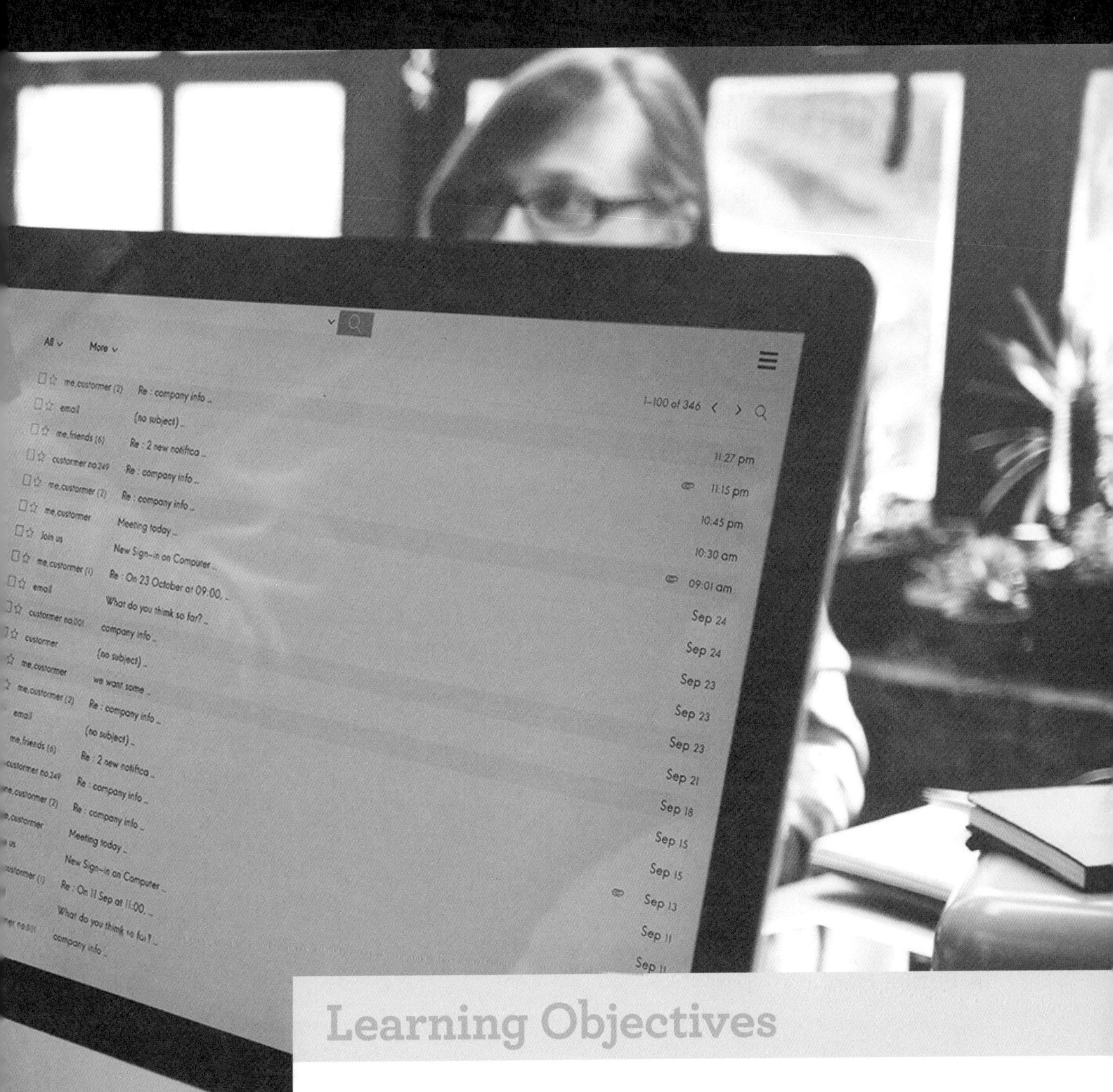

Learning Objectives

Upon completion of the unit, students will be able to:

- tell the differences between formal and informal emails;
- write business emails in formal and informal ways;
- make appropriate respond to emails.

Starting Off

1 Answer the questions.

1) Do you prefer to use the phone or to communicate by email, web chat or text message? Why?

2) Think about the emails that you receive. Which do you find easy to understand and which ones are difficult? Can you identify features of clear and unclear emails?

Messages A

2 Read and repeat.

A First Contact

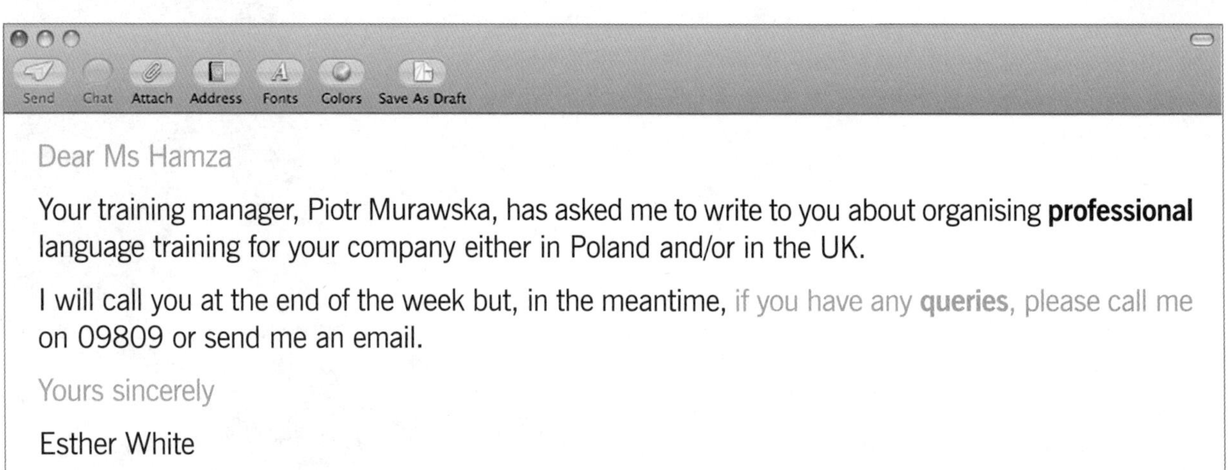

Dear Ms Hamza

Your training manager, Piotr Murawska, has asked me to write to you about organising **professional** language training for your company either in Poland and/or in the UK.

I will call you at the end of the week but, in the meantime, if you have any **queries**, please call me on 09809 or send me an email.

Yours sincerely

Esther White

A Future Meeting

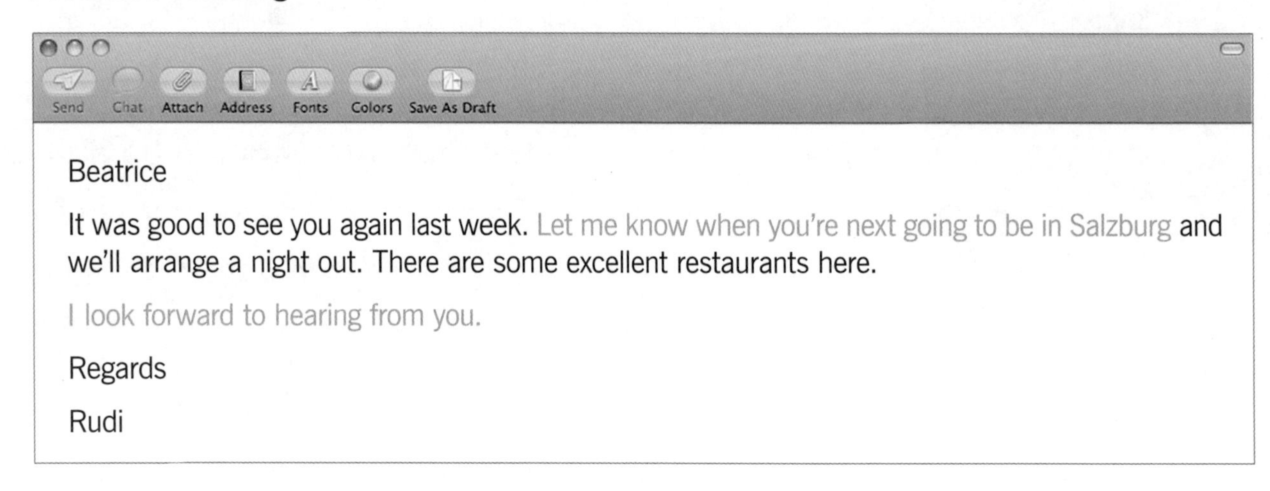

Beatrice

It was good to see you again last week. Let me know when you're next going to be in Salzburg and we'll arrange a night out. There are some excellent restaurants here.

I look forward to hearing from you.

Regards

Rudi

Everyday Matters

Hi Jaana

Hope you're feeling better. I heard from Jack that you had **flu**.

I'm sorry to say that I have a problem next week. Tina's on holiday and I have to **cover** for her so I won't be able to see you on Thursday. I'll call you later and we can arrange an **alternative** date.

Speak to you later

Ian

A Formal Message

Dear Colleague

I am writing to inform you and your staff that we are **relocating** our offices to Pisa. We will close on 2 November and will reopen in our new **premises** on 1 December.

We will contact you again in the near future.

Best regards

Duncan Hoe

MY GLOSSARY

professional	*adj.*	专业的; 职业的
query	*n.*	疑问, 问题
flu	*n.*	流行性感冒, 流感
cover	*v.*	代替, 顶替
alternative	*adj.*	可替代的, 可供选择的
relocate	*v.*	搬迁, 迁移
premises	*n.*	经营场所, 办公场所

Useful Expressions

Dear Ms Hamza

– Use *Dear* with the person's title and surname when you have not written to the person before or when you have a formal relationship. If you are in doubt, it is better to be more, rather than less formal.

...if you have any queries, please call me...

– This expression is quite often used at the end of an email. Also:

If you have any questions, please call me.

Yours sincerely

– In formal emails, we can use the formal letter-writing expressions:

Start: *Dear Ms/Mr/Mrs Pringle*

End: *Yours sincerely*

Start: *Dear Sir/Madam*

End: *Yours faithfully*

Let me know when you're next going to be in Salzburg...

– A friendly note to end. Some alternatives:

You must visit us again soon.

It was great to see you.

See you again soon.

I look forward to hearing from you.

– Note that we say:

I look forward to hearing from you. Although quite formal, *look forward to* is very often used in emails. Also common:

I look forward to meeting/seeing you.

Hi Jaana

– *Hi* is a common informal way to begin an email. You can also say "Hello Jaana". Use a person's name or say something like "Good morning" or "Good afternoon". Personalise your messages.

Hope you're feeling better.

– Some other opening expressions:

Just to let you know that...

Sorry to hear about…

Thanks for the message.

…I have to cover for her…

– *Cover for* means to do someone's job while the person is away.

Who's covering for you?

We're so short-staffed that there is no one to cover for me.

Speak to you later

– Expressions to indicate that you will be in contact later:

I'll send you a message later.

Call me when you get this message.

Dear Colleague

– The word *colleague* is used when writing to an identifiable group in more formal correspondence. It can be singular or plural. Note also:

Dear friend(s) / Dear member(s) / Dear All / Dear Sir/Madam (when you do not know the name of the person you are writing to)

I am writing to inform you…

– Full verb forms (for example, *I am writing*) are often used in formal communication. Note the less formal (and more common) alternatives:

I am writing (I'm writing) to inform you…

I am sure (I'm sure) that we can be of help…

I will call (I'll call) you at the end of the week.

We will (We'll) contact you again.

Best regards

– *(With) best regards* is a very common way to end an email and can be used in formal and informal contexts. There are many other ways to end:

Regards / Best wishes / Yours / All the best

British	**American**
If you have any queries…	The term queries is not used as frequently in American English as it is in British English.
Yours sincerely	*Sincerely*

Messages B

3 Read and repeat.

Saying Thank You (1)

Fred

Many thanks for helping with the conference. I'm very sorry that so few people came on Saturday—let's not organise the final **session** in the middle of a public holiday next year.

Anyway, let's hope we have better luck in Yokohama.

Take care

Lucy

Saying Thank You (2)

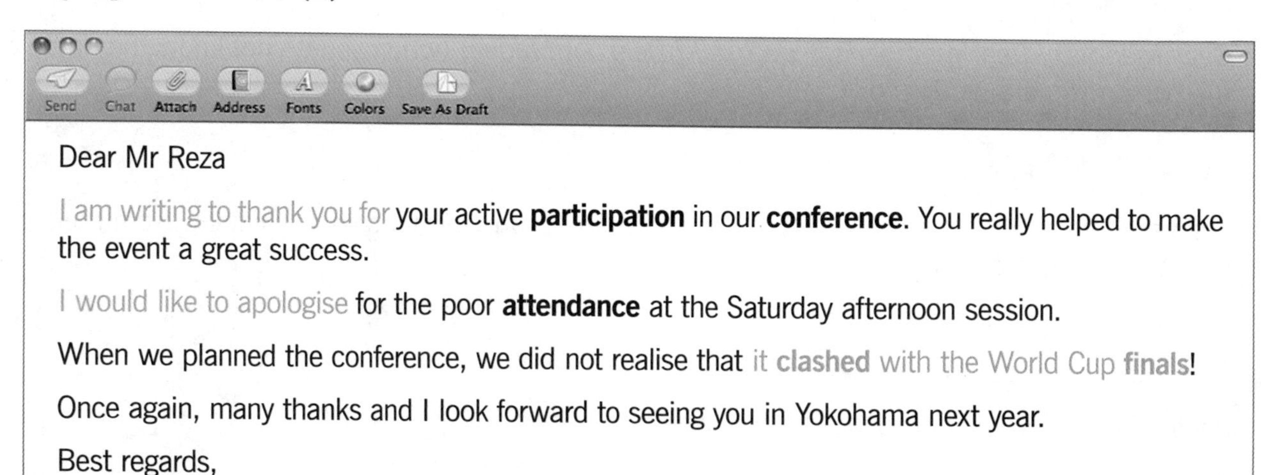

Dear Mr Reza

I am writing to thank you for your active **participation** in our **conference**. You really helped to make the event a great success.

I would like to apologise for the poor **attendance** at the Saturday afternoon session.

When we planned the conference, we did not realise that it **clashed** with the World Cup **finals**!

Once again, many thanks and I look forward to seeing you in Yokohama next year.

Best regards,

Lucy Lo Kit

An Invitation

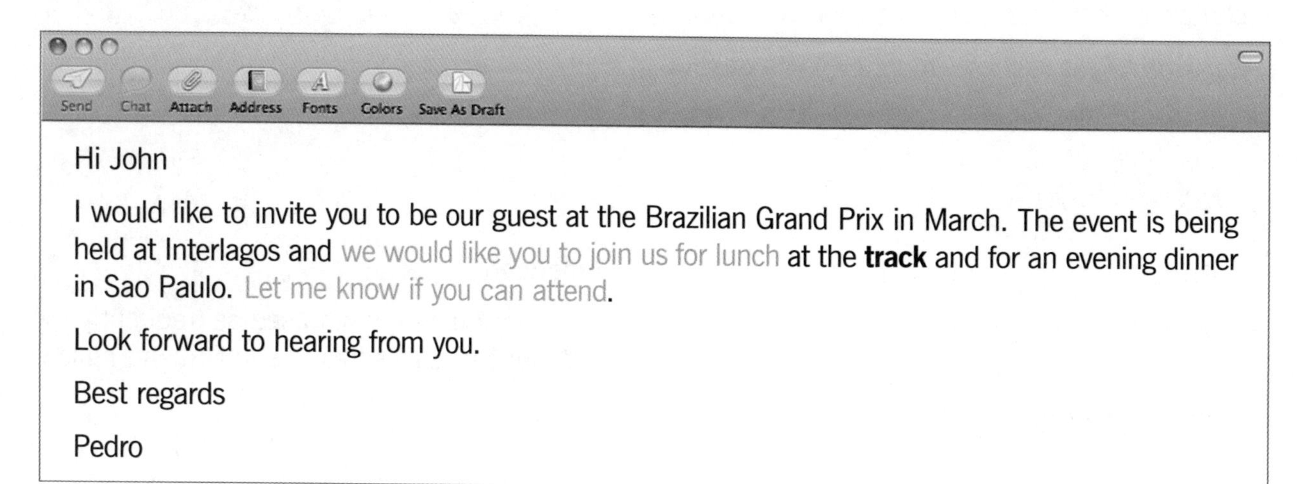

Hi John

I would like to invite you to be our guest at the Brazilian Grand Prix in March. The event is being held at Interlagos and we would like you to join us for lunch at the **track** and for an evening dinner in Sao Paulo. Let me know if you can attend.

Look forward to hearing from you.

Best regards

Pedro

Accepting an Invitation

Pedro

Thanks for the invitation. I'd love to come and I look forward to seeing you then. Please send me details of the event when you have them.

Best regards

John

Declining an Invitation

Dear Pedro

Many thanks for your kind invitation to attend the Grand Prix. Unfortunately, I'll be abroad on that day and I won't be able to make it. I hope the event goes well for you and I look forward to seeing you soon.

With best regards

John

MY GLOSSARY

session	*n.*	会议；一场活动	clash	*v.*	冲突；矛盾
participation	*n.*	参加，参与	final	*n.*	决赛；期末考试
conference	*n.*	会议，大会	track	*n.*	赛道；跑道
attendance	*n.*	出席，参加	detail	*n.*	细节，详情

Useful Expressions

Many thanks for helping...

– Friendly informal thanks. Note also:

Once again, many thanks.

Very many thanks!

...a public holiday...

– In the UK, public holidays are called *bank holidays.*

Anyway, let's hope we have better luck in Yokohama.

– *Anyway* is often used when we want to make a different point, to move away from what we have just said:

Anyway, I don't want to think about it anymore.

Anyway, that's all I wanted to say.

Take care

– A phrase normally only used when talking to good friends. We do not use this phrase or others such as *Be good, Have fun!, Lucky you!* with our more formal business contacts!

I am writing to thank you for...

– Fairly formal language for saying thank you. Note also:

We really appreciate all your help.

We're very grateful for your help.

I would like to apologise...

– A formal way to apologise. A more informal expression:

I'm very/really sorry about it.

...it clashed with the World Cup finals!

– When two appointments in a diary *clash*, they happen at the same time.

...we would like you to join us for lunch...

– Note the other formal language used in this email. To be less formal, say:

Can you come to the Grand Prix?

I hope you can come to lunch.

Please come.

Let me know if you can attend.

– A less formal way to say this is:

Let me know if you can make it.

I'd love to come...

– An informal enthusiastic response to an invitation. Some others:

That would be great.

That's a great idea.

I'll really look forward to it.

Please send me details of the event...

– An event is a special occasion.

It's going to be a very special event.

It took a long time to plan the event.

Many thanks for your kind invitation...

– Using a word such as *kind* emphasises the warmth of the thank you:

It was very kind of you to invite me.

– Other ways of saying thank you:

Thank you for your excellent presentation.

Many thanks for the beautiful flowers.

Unfortunately, I'll be abroad...

– You can avoid saying sorry by using *unfortunately*:

Unfortunately, I'm going to miss the presentation.

I won't be there, unfortunately.

I hope the event goes well for you…

– A friendly remark when you cannot attend a meeting or event:

I hope it all goes well.

Good luck with everything.

I hope I'll be able to come next time.

British	**American**
realise	*realize*
bank holiday	*legal/national/public holiday*

Messages C

4 Read and repeat.

Problems

Dear Serge

I have just heard from our French office that they are having problems arranging the meeting in Paris next week. There is a problem with **accommodation** as there is a large trade fair on at that time. All the hotels are full. Do you have any suggestions?

Best regards

Emilia

Good News

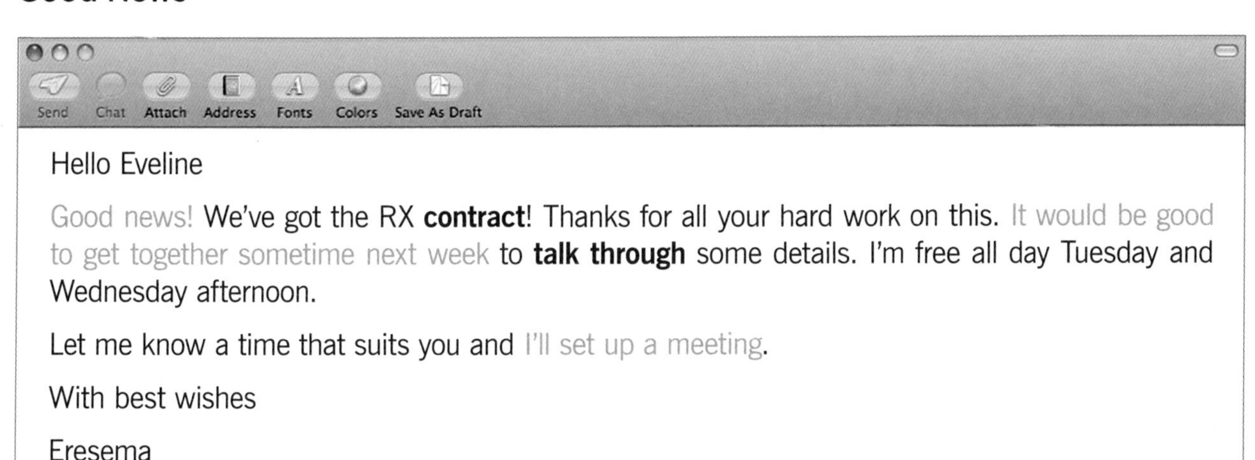

Hello Eveline

Good news! We've got the RX **contract**! Thanks for all your hard work on this. It would be good to get together sometime next week to **talk through** some details. I'm free all day Tuesday and Wednesday afternoon.

Let me know a time that suits you and I'll set up a meeting.

With best wishes

Eresema

A General Announcement

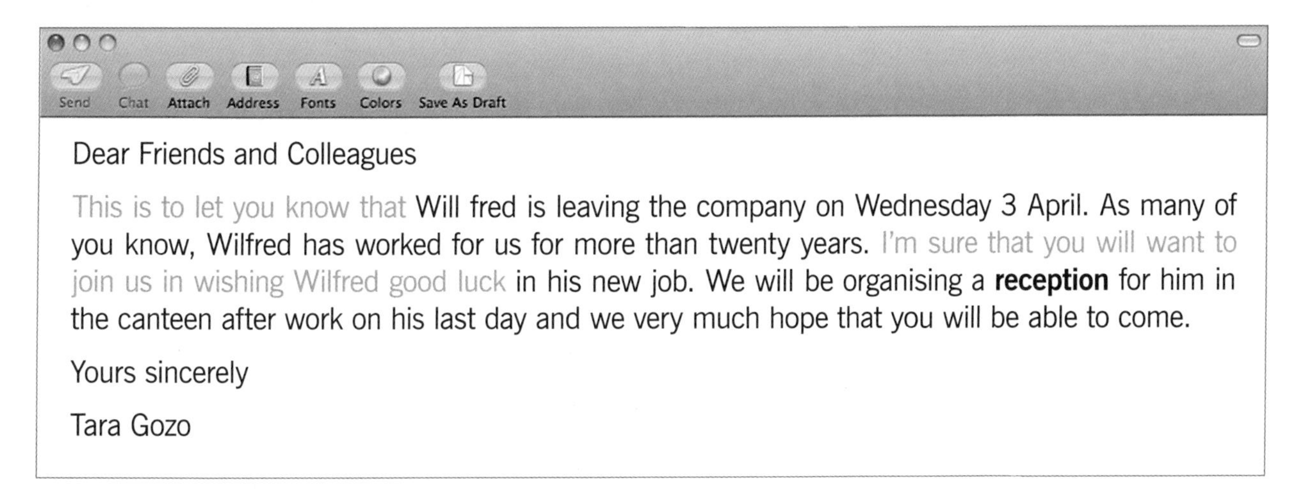

Dear Friends and Colleagues

This is to let you know that Will fred is leaving the company on Wednesday 3 April. As many of you know, Wilfred has worked for us for more than twenty years. I'm sure that you will want to join us in wishing Wilfred good luck in his new job. We will be organising a **reception** for him in the canteen after work on his last day and we very much hope that you will be able to come.

Yours sincerely

Tara Gozo

For Information

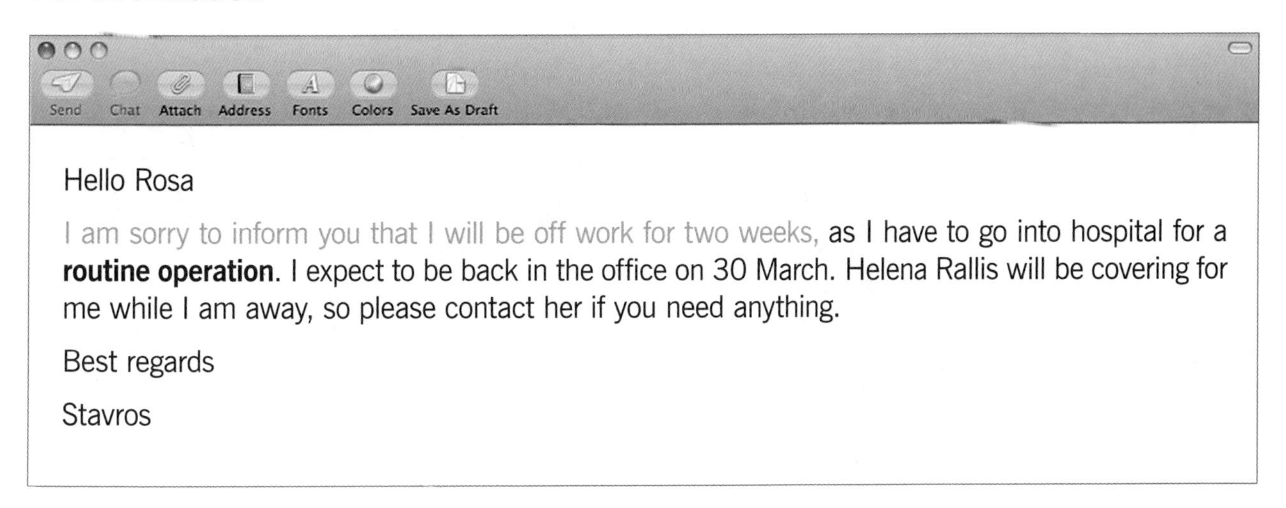

Hello Rosa

I am sorry to inform you that I will be off work for two weeks, as I have to go into hospital for a **routine operation**. I expect to be back in the office on 30 March. Helena Rallis will be covering for me while I am away, so please contact her if you need anything.

Best regards

Stavros

Passing on Good Wishes

Hi Helena

I was sorry to hear about Stavros. I am sure that he is keen to get back to work but tell him to **take his time**!

Please pass on my best wishes.

Regards

Rosa Fuente

MY GLOSSARY

accommodation	*n.*	住处，膳宿
contract	*n.*	合同，契约
talk through		详细讨论
announcement	*n.*	通知
reception	*n.*	欢送会；招待会
routine	*adj.*	常规的，平常的；例行的
operation	*n.*	手术；经营
take one's time		不着急，慢慢来

Useful Expressions

...they are having problems arranging the meeting...

– Problems and difficulties:

We're having some difficulties.

There's a problem.

It's difficult to arrange.

Do you have any suggestions?

– Looking for a solution:

Any ideas?

Do you have any ideas?

How can we sort it out?

How can we solve the problem?

Good news!

– Some enthusiastic responses to good news:

What good news!

That's great news!

That's fantastic/excellent news!

It would be good to get together sometime next week...

– *Get together* means to meet. (A *get-together* is an informal meeting, maybe a party). Other ways to suggest a meeting:

Let's meet next week.

Let's meet up in the near future.

We must arrange to meet up soon.

...I'll set up a meeting.

– Another way of saying this:

I'll arrange/organise a meeting.

This is to let you know that...

– Use *This is* in formal messages to refer to the message you are sending:

This is to inform you that the package will be late.

This is to remind you to call Vera.

– Informal alternatives:

Just to let you know that the package will be late.

I'm just writing to say that...

I'm sure that you will want to join us in wishing Wilfred good luck...

– Note the use of *join* in formal messages.

I hope you can join us for dinner.

Please join us in the evening if you can.

I am sorry to inform you that...

– Less formal:

Sorry to tell you that...

I'm writing to let you know that...

I'm afraid I have some bad news.

...I will be off work for two weeks,...

– Some alternative expressions:

She'll be on sick leave.

She'll be away from work.

She'll be at home.

I was sorry to hear about Stavros.

– Expressions of sympathy:

I was very sad to hear the news.

Everyone was very upset about it.

We'll miss him.

Please pass on my best wishes.

– Some other sympathetic expressions:

I'll be thinking of him.

We hope he gets well soon.

Please pass our sincere condolences to his family. (when someone has died)

British	American
go into hospital	*go into the hospital*
How can we sort it out?	*How can we figure it out?*

Technical Terms

premises the land and buildings owned by a company or an institution in one place 经营厂所; 办公场所

Grand Prix one of a series of important international races for very fast and powerful cars 国际汽车大奖赛, 汽车拉力赛

trade fair a large event at which companies show and sell their products and try to increase their business 商品交易会

Practice

1 Complete each sentence with the correct preposition.

1) She's ___on___ sick leave.
2) We will contact you again ________ the near future.
3) I look forward ________ hearing from you.
4) I'll call you ________ the end of the week.
5) Please call me ________ 456789.
6) Many thanks ________ all your help.
7) Good luck ________ everything.
8) I'm covering ________ Raj while he is away.
9) He will be ________ work for two weeks due to illness.
10) Please pass ________ our best wishes to him.

2 Some of these expressions are used formally and some informally. Tick the correct column.

	a	b	formal	informal
1)	Dear John	Hi John	☐	☐
2)	I am writing to inform you that...	I'm writing to let you know that...	☐	☐
3)	We're having a get-together.	We're arranging a meeting.	☐	☐
4)	I would like to apologise for	Sorry about...	☐	☐
5)	Let me know if you can make it.	Let me know if you can attend.	☐	☐
6)	I would be very pleased to come.	I'd love to come.	☐	☐

3 Write the sentences in this letter in the correct order.

Dear Mr Green

a ☐ Members of our sales team will present the service
b ☐ After the presentation
c [1] We would like to invite you to the launch of
d ☐ and there will be an opportunity to ask questions.
e ☐ there will be dinner in the main restaurant.
f ☐ our new courier service on 6 March

g ☐ I very much hope that you can attend.

h ☐ at the Grand Hotel at 6:30 p.m.

Best regards

Peter Pod

4 Complete the sentences with the verbs from the box. Use each verb once only.

miss	~~inform~~	must	hope	pass	join	call	get	thank	write

1) I'm writing to *inform* you that the conference has been cancelled.
2) Your training manager has asked me to ______ to you.
3) I'll ______ you at the end of the week.
4) I ______ you're feeling better.
5) You ______ visit us again soon.
6) I'd like to ______ you for all your hard work.
7) Please ______ us for lunch on 19 November.
8) Can we ______ together sometime next week?
9) I'm sorry Peter has left. We'll all ______ him.
10) We were very sad to hear about Hubert. Please ______ on our condolences.

5 Match the two parts of the sentences.

1) I am sorry to inform you that I
2) I'll call you when I
3) Let me know when you are next
4) I'd like to thank you for
5) I look forward to
6) I hope that the party
7) Unfortunately, the event clashes with
8) It was very kind of you

a ☐ hearing all your news.
b ☐ goes well.
c ☐ all your help.
d ☐ (going to be) in London.
e *1* will be out of the office next week.
f ☐ to invite me.
g ☐ get back to Cairo.
h ☐ an important meeting.

6 Rewrite the phrases and sentences in a less formal way.

1) Dear Tomas

Hi Tomas / Hello Tomas / Tomas

2) We will contact you in the near future.

3) We would like to thank you for organising the conference.

4) This is to inform you that we have changed the date of the meeting.

5) Please let us know if you can attend.

6) We trust that you will be able to join us for dinner.

7) I will call you at the end of the week.

8) We wish you every success in the future

9) We are organising a party next week.

7 Complete the sentences. The first letters of the missing words have been given.

1) It would be g *reat* ______ if you could come to the party!
2) Please pass on my best w ______ to everyone.
3) I would like to a ______ for the problems with the arrangements.
4) Please t ______ care!
5) We are organising a special p ______ at the end of the year. You must come!
6) I look f ______ to hearing from you.
7) I can't come to the party, u ______.
8) Let's hope we have better l ______ next time.

8 Suppose you are Mr Green. Write a reply to Mr Peter Pod's email in Exercise 3 declining his invitation. Remember to give reasons and thanks appropriately.

Send Chat Attach Address Fonts Colors Save As Draft